PHOTOSHOP
IN BLACK AND WHITE
2ND EDITION

JIM RICH AND SANDY BOZEK

Peachpit Press

CREDITS

Editing: Amy Lee, Ambrose Liao

Book Design/Illustration: Sandy Bozek

Cover Design: The Visual Group

Special thanks to:

Adobe Systems Inc. - Rita Amladi, Bryan Lamkin

AGFA - Jackie Group, Robin O'Leary

Baltimore ColorPlate - Randy Dorman, Franz Heinzerling, and Eli Renn

The Lanman Companies - Harry Knapman, Bill Dingle

Montgomery College - Fred Howell

Other individuals - Charlie Ashton, Brian Bassindale, Matt Brown, Elizabeth Dickerson, Joe Emrich, Steve Hannaford, Tim Helsing, Scott Kramer, Mike Lee, Don McFall, Kevin Ness, Cindy Marcotty, Mark Muse, Jeff Parker, Miles Southworth, Carmen Strollo, Michael Stoianovci, Glen Talmadge, Chuck Weger, and Tim Windsor

Photos: NASA

Scanning: AGFA Arcus Plus, Sharp JX600, Microtek 600ZS

Imagesetting: AGFA SelectSet 7000

PHOTOSHOP IN BLACK AND WHITE 2ND EDITION
Jim Rich and Sandy Bozek

PEACHPIT PRESS
2414 Sixth Street
Berkeley, CA 94710
(800) 283-9444
(510) 548-4393
(510) 548-5991 Fax

Peachpit Press is a division of Addison-Wesley Publishing Company.

NOTICE OF LIABILITY:

TRADEMARKS:

ISBN: 1-56609-189-6

Printed in the United States of America.

PREFACE

Photoshop isn't just for color photo retouching. It has dozens of tools that enable the user to correct and enhance photos of any type. Just think, no more big bills from the photo lab. No more tears about the perfect shot that was over or under exposed. You have the hardware, you have the software. Use Adobe Photoshop to take charge of your black-and-white images!

Our goal is to explain how to: use the tools in Adobe Photoshop to adjust the tones of black-and-white images for reproduction purposes; relate the tools to conventional methods for producing quality images; and establish a method for the user to achieve consistent quality results. We use print as the example for reproducing images but the reproduction concepts of the book easily apply to output for digital photography and multimedia.

This book is **NOT** about special effects, image retouching, design, or page assembly.
(It's much too thin for all of that.)

You will need the following experience to use this book successfully:

• Understand the basic commands of point, click, drag, open, close, and save.

• Be able to open or scan an image into Adobe Photoshop.

• Have the minimum system requirements for the program.

• Have a basic knowledge of the menu structure of Adobe Photoshop.

The differences between Adobe Photoshop for the Macintosh and Adobe Photoshop for IBM PC and compatibles are minimal. The tools work identically. The main differences are in the dialog boxes. Adobe Photoshop's dialog boxes on the PC platform incorporate a Help Menu, whereas those on the Macintosh version of Photoshop do not. There are one or two other instances where the PC version of Photoshop varies and they are noted with a **PC** symbol.

At the end of the book you will find two appendices that go into further technical detail about desktop scanning and calibration. We realize that no one (including us) likes to read a lot of technical stuff but after you have used the techniques outlined in the beginning of this book, and have gained more experience in using them, you might like to read some of the more detailed information about the process of creating quality black-and-white images. Now go into that closet at the back of your office or reach deep into that desk drawer, find the good photos and the bad ones that you couldn't bear to throw away and learn to work a little magic!

Jim Rich & Sandy Bozek
Annapolis, Maryland

CONTENTS

1

INTRODUCTION TO THE HALFTONE REPRODUCTION PROCESS

The **reproduction process** starts after an original scene is captured on continuous-tone film (the material you load into your camera). The continuous-tone film is converted, via an input scanner, into a digital signal that represents the original black-and-white image. The black-and-white digital information is optimized, converted into a file for output, and halftone film and a proof are generated.

After the review process, the proof is approved or is sent back to the workstation for adjustments. Once the adjustments are approved, printing plates are made from the halftone film. The plates are placed on a printing press and your image is printed.

Images are available with two types of characteristics: (1) continuous tone and (2) line work.

Continuous-tone images have a broad range of tones that do not use screened dots. They can be black-and-white (grayscale) or color and can come from transparencies or reflection originals.

Transparent originals are available in two forms: positives or negatives. Positive transparencies allow light to pass through and they appear similar to the original scene (like slides). Positive film comes in different sizes from 16 mm to over 20" x 24". Negatives are the transparent plastic strips you get back from the store with your prints that show a reverse of the image.

Black-and-white and color **reflective** originals reflect light off of their surfaces. We're talking about the basic photographic print. Much like transparencies, photographic reflection prints or originals come in many different sizes. Reflection originals range in size from 35 mm contact prints to any size painting or artwork.

Line Work images have two tonal values (black and white) and are suitable for reproduction without a halftone screen.

Graphic arts scanners are specialized high resolution drum and flatbed devices. Graphic arts scanners can provide the necessary features such as the final resolution (dpi), screen frequency (LPI) and sharpness functions necessary to reproduce black-and-white images. This group of scanners provide options for the final image to be output directly to final halftone film or as an electronic file to be used at a workstation.

Desktop and Plug-'n-Play Scanning involves more than the scanner. It includes the use of a workstation with specialized software (Adobe Photoshop!) and an imagesetter. The purpose of the desktop scanner is to capture grayscale or color digital data that can be adjusted and optimized at the workstation and output via an imagesetter.

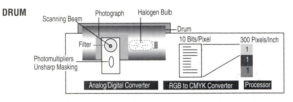

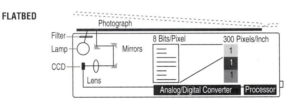

A bit is the smallest unit of data a computer uses. It has 2 states: 1(on) or Ø (off) (1 Bit)

$1 \text{ bit} = 2^1 = 2 \text{ shades}$

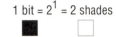

$8 \text{ bit} = 2^8 = 256 \text{ shades}$

With 8 bits and 2 states you can make 256 combinations of the 8 bits

1Ø1Ø1111(8 Bits)

In an 8 bit file each pixel (picture element) can contain 1 of the 256 shades or RGB levels

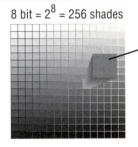

Scanners can output RGB (Red, Green and Blue) and CMYK, (Cyan, Magenta, Yellow, and Black) or grayscale digital data. RGB data values are measured in levels from 0-255. CMYK and grayscale data are measured in % of dot values ranging from 0% to 100%. Each level equals .39 of a dot %. In a grayscale reproduction the RGB levels are equal to each other.

Digital Data gathered during input scanning describes the original's tonal characteristics and resolution. The data is stored as a series of bits that define pixels for display on a computer monitor. The number of bits identifies the scanner sensor's capability to capture tonal information. To reproduce a grayscale continuous-tone image, 8 bits per pixel (256 levels) are required. Line art only requires 1 bit per pixel (two levels).

Laser Proof- adequate for concept and position.

Contact Print - Used as contract proof but does not reflect dot gain.

Matchprint™/Cromalin™ - Used as contract proof. Can show effects of dot gain. Produced from film.

Digital Proof - Used as contract proof. Can show effects of dot gain. Made before film.

Proofs are a visual "best guess" of the expected final reproduction. Some proofs are closer to the final end product than others. The more exact the proof, the more expensive it is to produce. The more exact proofs are usually saved for the end of the reproduction process. They can be created digitally or made with the film output from the imagesetter. When a client "OK's" the proof it becomes a contract between them and the party that supplied the proof (you). When you "OK" the proof to the printer the same implied contract exists.

Tone Compression occurs because the range of reproducible tones in the printing process is smaller than the range of tones of the original image. The original image contains a smaller range than you see in real life. Due to the effects of tone compression, images with average, light, or dark characteristics have their own special adjustments applied during the scanning process or on the desktop to achieve optimum results.

Dot Gain causes halftone dot sizes to increase. Dot gain can come from imagesetter miscalibration, varying paper qualities, and mechanical limitations of the printing process. Dot gain can adversely change the look of your final printed image.

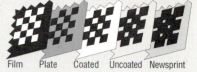

Film   Plate   Coated   Uncoated   Newsprint

PPI (Pixels Per Inch), DPI (Dots Per Inch), and LPI (Lines Per Inch), are all units of measure. These units apply to digital data and relate to the ability of specialized hardware to capture and use that digital data. Monitors display individual dots of light or Pixels (picture elements) on screen to form an image. An image needs to have a higher DPI for printing than it does to look good on a monitor. DPI represents the resolution of a device. Typical resolutions are 72-77 DPI for a monitor, 300-3000+ DPI for scanners and imagesetters. DPI and PPI are often used interchangeably. LPI refers to a line screen ruling used in halftone reproduction to simulate various shades of gray.

Calibration occurs when all hardware and software components throughout the process predictably produce standardized values and measures. In other words, you get no (or very few) surprises when you compare your proofs to the final printed image. During the reproduction process, scanned image values, values in the workstation, and image output values interrelate and agree. Calibration is the process by which the input and output values are adjusted to compensate for miscalibrated imagesetters, the varying properties of paper and ink, and different printing presses (see Dot Gain).

Pixels   Halftone Dots

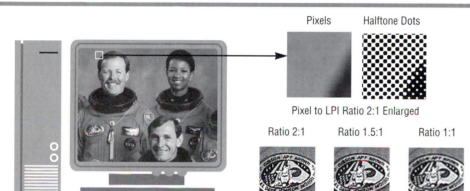

Pixel to LPI Ratio 2:1 Enlarged

Ratio 2:1   Ratio 1.5:1   Ratio 1:1

Best Quality   Good Quality   Some Uses

At 300 DPI a 133 ls yields 5 shades of gray

At 1200 DPI a 133 ls yields 81 shades of gray

At 2400 DPI a 133 ls yields 256 shades of gray

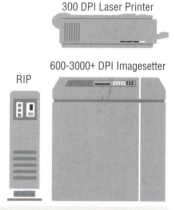

To ensure the best reproduction quality, the line screen (ls) and imagesetter resolution should be chosen to produce 256 shades of gray, the maximum addressable in the PostScript language.

300 DPI Laser Printer

600-3000+ DPI Imagesetter

RIP

Workstations are powerful computer systems that enable the user to make adjustments to digital images to optimize their reproduction and to perform imaging functions like cloning, airbrushing, and retouching. Workstation platforms include Unix, IBM-PC and compatibles, and Apple Macintosh.

Halftones are used to reproduce continuous-tone images on a printing press. A halftone line screen (LS) divides an image into patterns of different-sized dots that create an optical illusion of continuous shades of gray. To get the best results, an image needs to process through the imagesetter twice as many screen pixels as halftone dots at final image size. To produce the maximum levels of gray and reduce banding effects, the correct line screen and imagesetter resolution combination must be used. The number of available shades of gray is determined by the formula: # of shades = (Imagesetter output DPI/halftone screen LPI)^2 (squared) +1.

The **RIP** (Raster Image Processor) converts the digital data into the bitmap data the **Imagesetter** uses to render line work or halftone information onto film or paper. A 300 DPI laser printer is a low resolution imagesetter.

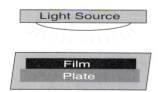

Light Source

Film

Plate

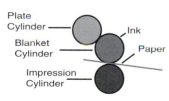

Plate Cylinder

Blanket Cylinder

Impression Cylinder

Ink

Paper

Original   Random Proof   Printed Piece

Printing involves rendering the image data to a substrate such as paper. In the traditional printing process of offset lithography, halftone film generated by imagesetters is photographically imaged onto printing plates. A plate is placed on a press, inked, and the halftone image is transferred to paper.

The Review Process is essential to determining if the reproduction is optimized. You do this by visually inspecting originals, proofs, and printed results and making judgments as to the degree of success you achieved in reproducing the image. If the image is not optimized, you can make future adjustments based on this inspection. Remember, experience is your best teacher.

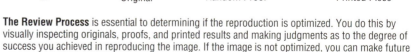

3

THE TOOLS

This section identifies the key tools that are used in Photoshop when producing black-and-white images.

ITEM LOCATOR

To aid in finding the tools in this section, we have added a guide to the headings. When you see a heading like this:

GENERAL `File: Preferences`

It indicates that the item General is found under the menu bar selection File and then under Preferences.

PHOTOSHOP TOOLBOX (F.Y.I.)

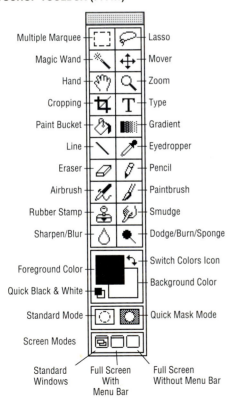

Multiple Marquee — Lasso
Magic Wand — Mover
Hand — Zoom
Cropping — Type
Paint Bucket — Gradient
Line — Eyedropper
Eraser — Pencil
Airbrush — Paintbrush
Rubber Stamp — Smudge
Sharpen/Blur — Dodge/Burn/Sponge

Foreground Color — Switch Colors Icon
Quick Black & White — Background Color

Standard Mode — Quick Mask Mode

Screen Modes

Standard Windows — Full Screen With Menu Bar — Full Screen Without Menu Bar

GENERAL `File: Preferences`

General Preferences contains several settings choices that affect the reproduction of grayscale images. Set the Interpolation to Bicubic for more accurate calculations. Turn on Video LUT (Look Up Table) Animation. If your video board cannot use Video LUT Animation, use the Preview button to view changes to the image on screen. Check with your video card manufacturer if you have specific questions about LUT Animation. Also, be sure to select the Photoshop Color Picker or you will be unable to select the K value (black) in the CMYK value boxes in the Color Pickers.

PRINTING INKS SETUP `File: Preferences`

Printing Inks Setup was not previously used for grayscale work, but in Adobe Photoshop 2.5 and later, a check box was added to allow you to preview changes due to dot gain variations. However, this feature may not function as expected. Depending on the dot gain value and the check box status, the RGB values in the Info palette can display incorrectly, or the incorrect values are set when using the Set White, Set Black, and Auto adjustment features of Levels and Curves. We recommend that you use the settings shown here if you want the RGB values in the Info palette to display correctly and if you want the Levels and Curves tools to work correctly.

MONITOR SETUP `File: Preferences`

These settings have no effect on how grayscale images will actually print UNLESS you leave the "Use Dot Gain for Grayscale Images" UNCHECKED in the Printing Inks Setup dialog box. We recommend that you leave the Use Dot Gain set up as indicated above. The Gamma and the Room Parameters do affect how the image will display. These should be based on the settings used in your calibration software or the settings chosen when you use the Gamma control panel which is included with Photoshop. See the Calibration section on page 33 for further details.

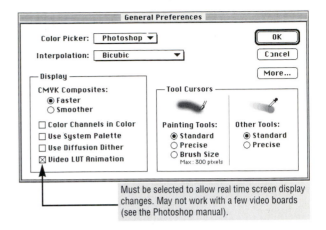

Must be selected to allow real time screen display changes. May not work with a few video boards (see the Photoshop manual).

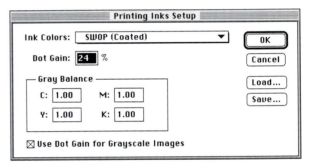

Use these settings to ensure that the tools work as expected !

EYEDROPPER TOOL `Window: Palettes:`

This is one of the key tools for measuring. It is used in conjunction with Curves or Levels to identify highlight (white) and shadow (black) areas. Double clicking on this tool in the Toolbox brings up a dialog box for the eyedropper sample size. The default "Point Sample," samples only one pixel in a given area and you may end up with a single, non representative pixel being read, measured, and used for calculations. The preferred setting is 3 by 3 average, which increases the sample size and minimizes erroneous readings.

Double click on the Eyedropper tool icon to access the Eyedropper Options dialog box in the Options Pal

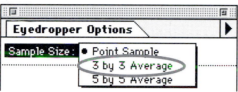
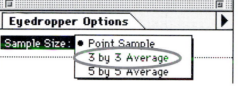

COLORS PALETTE `Window: Palettes:`

This tool permits sampling of any area within an image in digital RGB or halftone dot values. The Colors Palette is used by clicking on an image area with the eyedropper tool. The value selected is displayed in either the foreground or background color box in the palette. The values in the Colors Palette dialog box will stay displayed until another area is clicked. The Scratch Pad is a separate Palette where you can use a draw tool to test a shade on the scratch pad area of the palette.

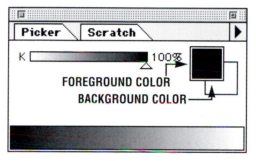

Option clicking with the eyedropper tool selects the background color

INFO PALETTE `Window: Palettes:`

This essential palette is a digital densitometer (see Glossary). It displays the X and Y pixel coordinates of the cursor, and the values for 5 color spaces. To use this tool for black-and-white images, set it for grayscale and RGB color spaces. The palette will display the image's dot percentages and RGB values (Levels) when the cursor is placed over a given image area. For example, when the palette indicates a 10% dot in a selected area of the image, the corresponding area of the output film will produce a 10% dot (providing the imagesetter is properly calibrated). The palette will display before and after values when making changes in the Curves and Levels dialog boxes.

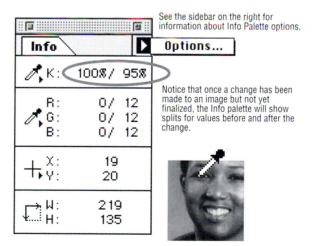

See the sidebar on the right for information about Info Palette options.

Notice that once a change has been made to an image but not yet finalized, the Info palette will show splits for values before and after the change.

OPTIONAL EYEDROPPER CURSOR

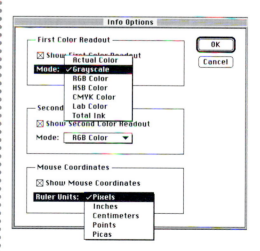

By locking the Shift key down when using this tool a target point cursor is displayed. This is an optional way to isolate specific points in the image.

INFO PALETTE OPTIONS

The color space or spaces displayed by the palette can be accessed and changed through the Options drop menu. It is also possible to change the Mouse Coordinates Ruler Units.

5

THE TOOLS
CONTINUED

SET WHITE/BLACK TARGET COLOR PICKER

This tool is used in conjunction with Curves or Levels to establish (or dial-in) the target highlight and shadow values of the image. (RGB values may also be used.) To enter the Color Picker when in Curves or Levels, double click the Set White or Set Black icon. Then, establish the highlight or shadow dot values. Be sure to place zeroes in the C, M, and Y boxes and click **OK**. A different Color Picker may also be accessed by clicking on the Foreground or Background box in the Tools palette. This picker looks the same as the Set White and Black pickers. However, it is not possible to set highlight and shadow points from the tool palette picker. Highlight and shadow points can **only** be set through their respective pickers in the Curves or Levels dialog box.

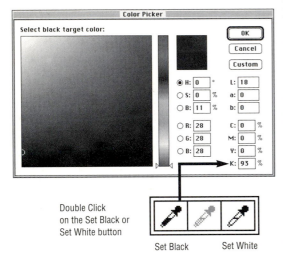

Double Click
on the Set Black or
Set White button

Set Black   Set White

IMPORTANT!

When establishing highlight and shadow values, use the k (black) channel only, be sure to enter zero values in the C, M, and Y channels.

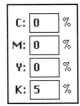

Highlight value   Shadow value

LEVELS `Image: Adjust`

This tool shows a Histogram that identifies the image characteristics by RGB levels (which range from 0 to 255). It has two sliding adjustment bars that allow you to change the input and output values. We have divided this tool into three adjustment classifications: manual, semi-automatic, and automatic.

■ With the **Manual** method, you sample areas with the eyedropper tool, read the values in the Info palette, and then adjust any or all of the five arrow sliders to make changes to meet reproduction requirements. This method requires a lot of expertise and can be very time consuming. If you choose to use the gamma (midtone) slider in the Levels dialog box, this adjustment is always done manually. Its use is covered in the How To section of this book.

■ The **Semi-Automatic** method uses the Set White and Set Black tools. You manually pick target highlight and shadow areas. This tool also allows you to visually locate the areas having the lightest or darkest pixels. You do this by holding down the Option key as you slide the right or left arrow below the input histogram back and forth. (The Preview option must be deselected and LUT Animation must be selected in the General Preferences for this effect to work.) **PC** Use the Alt key and click on the arrow.

■ The **Automatic** method requires that the white target and black target points be set in their respective Color Pickers. When you click on the Auto button, the program picks the white and black points in the image. While this method works, extraneous data in the photo such as borders or large dark or light areas can make it necessary to change the clip values to get the best results (see the sidebar, Clip Values, page 9).

Load and Save - These options are available for many of the adjustment tools. A particular setting can be saved, then loaded, and used on another image. This feature is helpful for repeating adjustments on images requiring similar changes thus speeding production.

Optimized Image

Histogram Display

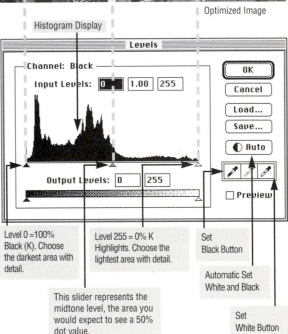

Level 0 =100% Black (K). Choose the darkest area with detail.

Level 255 = 0% K Highlights. Choose the lightest area with detail.

Set Black Button

Automatic Set White and Black

Set White Button

This slider represents the midtone level, the area you would expect to see a 50% dot value.

Load...   Save...

Manually adjusting Input Levels: This upper scale adjustment is used to change the current image input values to increase contrast. It does this by increasing the total number of light or dark pixels in the image.

For example, use a 16-step posterized ramp and move the Input Levels slider from level 0 to level 68.

The ramp now shows that there has been a dramatic increase in the number of the darkest pixels in the image. All pixels from level 68 and down have been assigned the maximum darkness value. By increasing the total number of dark and light pixels in an image, the contrast is increased. Notice also that the number of shade steps in the ramp has been reduced from 16 to 12. In a halftone, increasing contrast too far reduces the number of shades of gray and results in a posterized image.

After clicking **OK**, look at the histogram and notice the increase in number of darkest pixels and the redistribution of the other steps.

Manually adjusting Output Levels: The bottom scale is used to adjust or limit the lightest and darkest values in an image. For example, if the bottom left arrow slider is moved from 0 to 12 the image will not allow any values below 5% to be printed (level 12 is equal to a 95% dot value).

The example to the right was created using a 16-step posterized ramp. The left Input Levels slider is moved from level 0 to level 68 and the output has been limited to level 68.

Now the pixels from level 68 and down have been remapped to the darkest value allowed, but the darkest value allowed has been limited by the output limit slider to level 68. The resulting ramp shows less contrast. When used on a halftone image, the output slider should be used to limit the resulting image's darkest and lightest output values (i.e., to a 95% shadow dot and a 5% highlight dot). While this tool can be used to lower contrast in an image, it is most useful for limiting output values to a specific range.

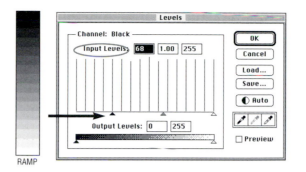

RAMP

RAMP

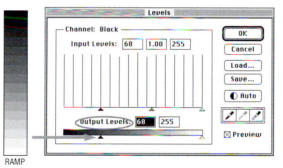

RAMP

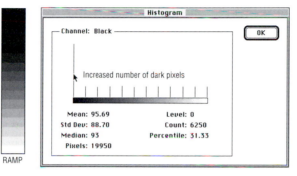

RAMP

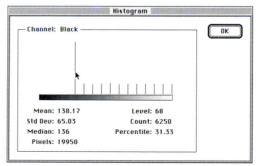

RAMP

MAKE YOUR OWN RAMPS

Experiment with the Levels tool to get the feel of it. Make a new file, 6" wide x 1" high. Select Grayscale, and 72 DPI. Then with the foreground color set to the default 100% black and the background color set to the default white, use the Gradient tool in the tool box to create a ramp like the one you see to the left. Then select Image: Map, Posterize from the menu and posterize it 16 levels (use 11 if you want even 10% increments, 21 if you want 5% increments). Now you have a ramp on which to try different adjustments with the Levels tool. Observe how different adjustments change the look of the ramp. This information can then be related to how this tool works with scanned images.

MIDTONE (GAMMA) ADJUSTMENT

The Levels tool has a midtone adjustment slider that ranges in value from .10 to 9.99 with the 1.0 value being an equal distance between the light and dark slider. A larger number increases the light tones in the image, and a smaller one decreases the light tones in the image. The Levels tool is limited since only three points of the reproduction are selectively adjustable: highlight, shadow, and midtones. While this is often sufficient, the Curves tool allows more than 3 points of the image's tones to be selectively adjusted.

EASY ENTRY FEATURE: DIAL-IN VALUE BOXES

Many dialog boxes can now accept values that are input directly into individual settings boxes rather than having to drag sliders to change values.

Input Levels: 0   1.00   255

THE TOOLS
CONTINUED

EXTREME EFFECTS OF MOVING CURVE ENDPOINTS

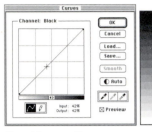

Normal Curve and image

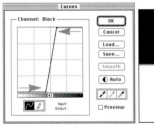

If the endpoints of the curve are moved as close to the vertical axis as possible, the resulting image is posterized (it gains the extreme contrast of a line art-type image).

When the two endpoints of the curve are moved closer to the horizontal axis, the result is a flat image. Adjusting the curve in this manner decreases contrast.

CURVES   Image: Adjust

The Curves dialog box, as its name suggests, allows adjustment of the image's tonal reproduction characteristics by adjusting a curve. Of the three tone reproduction adjustment tools, Curves is the most precise. It is possible to adjust specific areas of the tone such as midtone values, 1/4 tone values, 3/4 tone values, or multiple points along the curve. This is the traditional terminology used in the prepress field, making Curves the easiest tool to use when communicating specific "Dot" or % values for different types of paper and printing presses. Highlight (white) and shadow (black) settings are chosen in Curves via their respective Color Pickers.

The highlight and shadow adjustments with this tool, just like the Levels tool, can be divided into three classifications: manual, semi-automatic, and automatic.

- In **Manual** mode, sample an area with the eyedropper tool, read the value in the Color palette or Info palette, and then drag the end points of the curve manually to make changes to meet target tone reproduction requirements. This method requires a lot of expertise and can be very time consuming.

- The **Semi-Automatic** mode involves using the Set White and Set Black controls to define target values, and then manually selecting the target highlight and shadow areas. This tool also allows you to visually locate the area you have selected on the curve. This area is indicated by an open circle that appears on the curve. To get the circle, hold the mouse button down while the pointer is over the selected area on the image. (This is the method described in the How To section.)

- The **Automatic** method requires that the target White and Black point be set in the appropriate Color Picker. Clicking on the Auto button allows the program to pick the white and black points. (See the Auto Range options on the sidebar on page 9.)

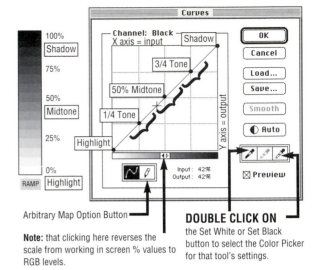

Arbitrary Map Option Button

Note: that clicking here reverses the scale from working in screen % values to RGB levels.

DOUBLE CLICK ON the Set White or Set Black button to select the Color Picker for that tool's settings.

Manually adjusting the end points of the curve

Input: Plotted on the X axis, this adjustment heightens contrast by increasing the total number of light or dark pixels in the image.

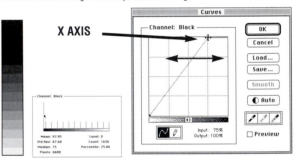

X AXIS

Output: The Y axis is used to set or limit the lightest and darkest values in an image. If the input and output values are set to 75%, the image will not have any values above 75%.

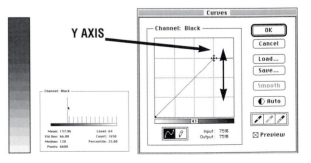

Y AXIS

Adjusting the midtones

There is no automatic adjustment for midtone values between the endpoints of the curve. To adjust a midtone area on the curve, move the cursor up to intersect a part of the line which forms the curve and click to place a point at that spot on the curve. You can then drag the point up or down to increase or decrease values in the image that are along the curve. When making adjustments with just one control point, the Curves tool works much like the Levels Gamma adjustment. The unique adjustment feature of the Curves tool is that it allows more than a single midtone control point. In fact, up to 14 additional points (besides the highlight and shadow anchors) can be placed along the curve allowing very specific areas of the tone to be changed without strongly affecting other areas. To prevent other tone areas from changing value, anchor those points on the curve.

The Curves tool display

When working in Curves, be sure that you have selected the % mode (unless you prefer levels) so that your adjustment looks like the first one on the right. You do this by clicking on the double arrow in the gradation bar. When in % mode, dragging a point down lightens an image. When working in Levels on the curve, dragging a point down darkens an image. You must drag the mouse in the image or have the cursor over an area in the curve to get the input and output values to display.

ARBITRARY MAP

Arbitrary Map is part of the Curves tool. To activate it, click on the pencil button at the bottom of the Curves dialog box. The cursor will change to a pencil when you draw inside the graph. The Arbitrary map tool can be used to make discontinuous changes to the curve. The Shift key can be used to constrain the lines drawn when the tool is clicked to define a specific start and end point along the curve. This tool can be particularly helpful when cleaning up scanned line art or when remapping a small number of pixels in a detailed area of an image.

Manually adjusting midtones on the curve

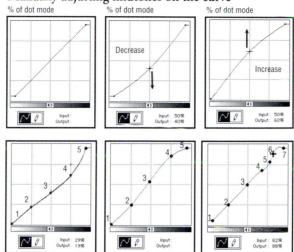

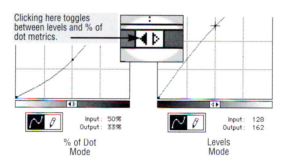

% of Dot
Mode

Levels
Mode

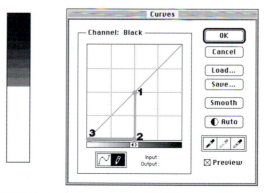

Change to ramp on page 6 made by holding the Shift key and clicking on points 1, 2, and 3.

THE AUTO BUTTON AND AUTO RANGE OPTIONS

This feature is used in conjunction with the Curves or Levels tool and requires that the proper white point and black point values be setup prior to using this tool. Hold down the Option key and click on the Auto button in either Curves or Levels. The Auto Range option dialog box is displayed with the default clipping values of 0.5%. This setting throws out the top and bottom 5% of the pixels used by the Auto tool equation before it calculates where to set White and Black points in an image.

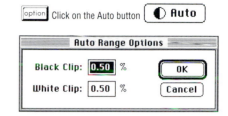

You might want to raise the clip value if there are large white or black areas in the image that you do not want to have used as part of the automatic calculation of the highlight and shadow points in the image. The clip values range from 0 to 9.99% so that the largest number of pixels at each end of the calculation range that can be removed from the calculation is about 10%.

In Photoshop 3.0, the Auto Levels feature has been added to the Image: Adjust menu so that it can be accessed by an F key or Command Menu. Remember the correct values must be dialed into the Set White and Set Black pickers for this feature to work.

PC Use the Alt key and click on the auto button.

BRIGHTNESS/CONTRAST

Brightness/Contrast is one of three basic image adjustment tools available in Adobe Photoshop. This tool works especially well for making adjustments to line work. However, in a comparison between Levels, Curves, and Brightness/Contrast for continuous-tone image adjustment, Brightness/Contrast provides the least amount of control because specific points of the image cannot be adjusted independently. So don't use it for halftones!

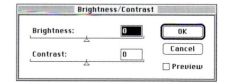

THE TOOLS
CONTINUED

HOW MANY GRAY LEVELS?

Quality black-and-white reproduction for print requires that the scanner be capable of capturing 256 levels of gray despite the fact that many images will not have all 256 levels.

THE HISTOGRAM IN THE LEVELS CONTROL

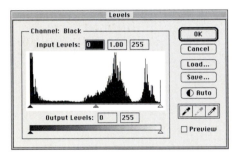

Notice, when using the Levels tool, a smaller version of the Histogram is provided to aid in adjusting the image values.

HISTOGRAM Image

The Histogram plots the number of pixels that are in a given level of the image. A level is the same as the RGB (Red, Green, and Blue) value displayed in the Info box for a given color. In the case of grayscale images, the RGB levels are equal because gray is defined as neutral (not cast or tinted with a hue). Additive color theory tells us that the RGB values must be equal to create a neutral value. The levels range from 0-255.

Using the Histogram

The Histogram provides a visual representation of the image, which permits a better understanding of the visual distribution of tones within the image. The Mean is an average of brightness values in a particular image. An image with a Mean value of around 128 usually identifies an image with an average distribution of tones. Images that have a Mean value range of 170 to 255 are light in character. Images that have a Mean value range of 85 to 0 are dark. Each of these image categories (light, average, and dark) follow basic guidelines for image adjustments. These adjustments are discussed in the section More About Midtones on page 22. The Histogram can be used to: categorize the image, determine the number of levels in the image, analyze the amount of data in each level, and view the result of adjustments to the image. The examples to the right illustrate the Histogram and how different types of scans or adjustments display in the histogram.

Placing the pointer at any single level in the Histogram displays information about that point. If there is no value at a selected level then no data exists at that point.

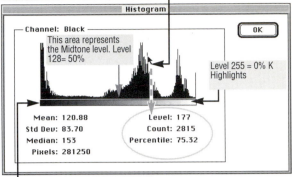

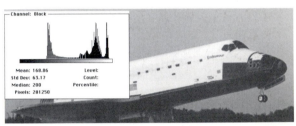

Histogram for a light scan. This scan was produced on an 8 bit scanner. Notice the densely packed tones.

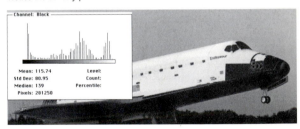

Histogram from an image scanned on a 4 bit scanner. Only 64 levels are available for adjustment.

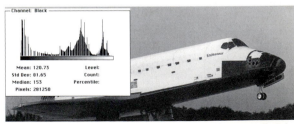

Histogram after the white point, the black point and the midtones are adjusted. The tones have distributed themselves more evenly.

PAGE SETUP `File`

The Page Setup dialog box has two important options that can be used with black-and-white images: the Halftone Screen Data and the Transfer Function. Use these if you need to override the halftone screen functions of your page layout program or if you want to compensate an individual halftone for a specific type of dot gain. To export this information, the file must be saved in EPS format.

Transfer Functions

The Adobe Photoshop manual indicates that the Transfer Function was "designed to compensate for dot gain due to a miscalibrated imagesetter." It qualifies the statement by stating that it is better to calibrate an imagesetter with specialized software recommended by the imagesetter manufacturer (we agree). We also use the Transfer Function to compensate for dot gain that occurs due to the different ink absorption rates of coated and uncoated papers, and the varied printing characteristics of specific types of printing presses. For example, a 50% dot on film might print like a 60% dot on coated paper (10% dot gain), and the same film might print like an 80% dot on newsprint (30% dot gain). If an image is being used for different purposes (i.e., a newspaper ad on newsprint and a high quality magazine ad on coated paper), the image will display different types of dot gain on each material. The specific curves can be created, saved, and loaded to be used again. It would be possible to set up curves specific to different vendors' needs without changing the original image. For more information on dot gain see page 35 in the appendix on Calibration.

Halftone Screen data

The desired line screen and the type of halftone dot can be selected from the Halftone Screen dialog box. This information, which can be saved only in EPS format, will override the settings in page layout programs. This is very useful if there is a need to use different screen rulings in the same document.

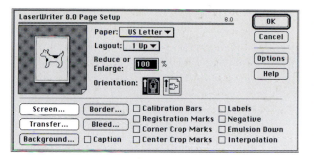

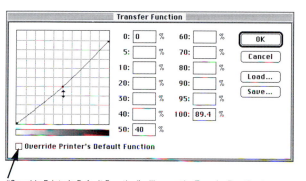

"Override Printer's Default Function" will cause the Transfer Function to override any other calibration software that is being used to calibrate the imagesetter. If it is not checked, the results of the transfer curve are additive to any calibration that is already being applied to the imagesetter.

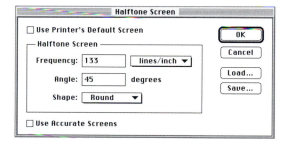

IMAGESETTER MISCALIBRATION

Imagesetter miscalibration occurs when the size of an uncompensated (no transfer function used) dot on the final film does not match the values indicated by the densitometer in the Info palette. An example would be if the Info palette indicated there should be a 50% dot and the film actually has a 69% dot. To determine the correct compensation value to plug into the 50% Transfer Function box, find the difference between 50% and 69% and subtract that difference from the original value. This value (31) is then placed in the 50% transfer curve box. That value will now compensate for the 19% dot gain. Continue this process with other dot percentages along the curve. Note: It is a good idea to verify that your film is being output on a calibrated imagesetter.

PRINTING TIP

Halftone dot % values can be remapped to another value to compensate for how a particular press or paper reacts and produces dot gain. It is important to work closely with the printer to determine the values they would like applied to a given image. A test strip can be run by producing rectangular areas with screens that vary in value from 5% to 95%. The printer can measure these values and then measure the dot percentages that are actually printed on the paper. The difference between the two values allows a transfer curve to be built and saved for specific situations.

A good set of basic transfer functions saved would include :

Web Press	Sheet-fed
Coated	Uncoated
Newsprint	LaserWriter

More can be added as needed.

SAVING A NEW DEFAULT:

To save a new default Halftone Line screen or Transfer Function, hold down on the Option key and click the –>Default button. To reset to the original setting, hold down on the Option key, and press <–Default.

With the Option key held down, the Load and Save buttons change as shown to the right.

11

THE TOOLS
CONTINUED

These filters provide different ways of making an image appear sharper by increasing the contrast between adjacent pixels. The Unsharp Mask command is the only filter with user controllable settings. Sharpen, Sharpen Edges, and Sharpen More can also be used but are not recommended since they are not adjustable. The Unsharp filtering effect increases contrast in the reproduction and makes it appear "sharper." Basically, it fools the eye into believing it is seeing greater detail by creating additional contrast and enhancing the differences between the light and dark transitions in an image.

WHEN UNSHARPENING ISN'T

The term Unsharp Masking (USM) comes from a conventional camera color separation technique that uses a piece of frosted mylar to make a photographic mask that the separation is exposed through. The result of this process is a separation with an increase in contrast in the reproduction giving it the illusion of sharpness. This term Unsharp Masking has been carried over to scanners and desktop computer software.

UNSHARP MASK ▐ Filter: Sharpen ▌

The Sharpen, Sharpen More, and Unsharp Mask filters produce sharpening effects that increase the contrast in adjacent pixels in a selection. The strongest and most controllable filter in this tool set is the Unsharp Mask (USM) filter.

Three parameters can be adjusted: **Amount, Radius,** and **Threshold.**

- **Amount** (USM relative value) ranges from 1% to 500%. Higher numbers produce stronger sharpening effects. Typically 150%-200% achieves good results.

- **Radius** values control the number of pixels around an image's edges that have sharpness applied. These values range from 0.1 to 99.99 pixels. If a high value is specified for the radius, more pixels around the edge pixels will be amplified. A typical setting of 1 to 2 pixels creates good contrast.

- **Threshold** acts as a mask that protects pixels from having USM applied. Values range between 0 and 255 The larger the value, the more an image area is protected from having USM applied. The value used to apply USM to the entire image is 0.

RULES OF THUMB FOR SHARPNESS

MEDIA
- Generally, original images such as 35mm and 4" x 5" originals require more sharpness than 2 1/4" x 2 1/4" transparencies. A 2 1/4" x 2 1/4" requires less sharpness since its thinner emulsion allows the image to be sharper from the start.
- Most second generation originals (dupes) are less sharp and require added sharpness.
- Reflection prints require less sharpness because the dyes in the prints are enhanced.

CONTENT
- Images with areas of great contrast differences require less added sharpness. Some examples are: different density areas adjacent to each other, dark lines against a light area such as telephone wires against a bright sky, window frames, and screen patterns.
- Images with fuzzy content require more added sharpness.
- Some images should be left un sharp, i.e., soft bridal shots or other artistic effects.

SIZE
- The greater the enlargement, the more sharpness is required.
- The smaller the enlargement or the greater the reduction, the less sharpness is needed.
- A 8.5" x 11" 300 dpi scan can take more sharpening than an 8.5 " x 5.5" 300 dpi scan.

Tip - The threshold value is a good tool to protect lighter tones. This is often useful for keeping some skin tone areas soft while sharpening the rest of the image. The example to the right shows values that can be used for creating this effect.

Image before Unsharp Mask

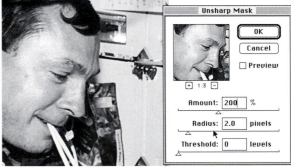

Image after Unsharp Mask 200, 1, 0

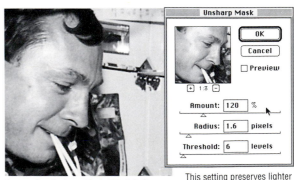

Image after Unsharp Mask 120, 1.6, 6

This setting preserves lighter flesh tones

THE REPRODUCTION PROCESS

A typical process for an image destined for publication in a brochure is to take the original continuous-tone, scan it to convert it to digital data, display the data via a workstation and a monitor, optimize the image, convert the digital data to halftone film dots, then print it on paper. The goal during the conversion process is to learn how to optimize each phase of the operation to produce predictable quality results. When this happens, the final result will be a good reproduction.

1. Examine the continuous-tone original

The first step in the process is to examine the original that is to be reproduced. It should be correctly exposed, have fine grain, and have good overall sharpness and contrast. If an image is lacking in any of these areas, additional corrections will need to be made to minimize any negative characteristics. Once you learn how to correct good quality originals, the same techniques can be used to improve bad images. But, some images may require using masking techniques and greater adjustments to achieve optimum results.

2. Scan the original

The next stage of the process is scanning. This converts continuous-tone data from photographic prints, slides or original art into digital data. For halftone reproduction, this data should be captured as a single grayscale channel, 3 RGB channels, or 4 CMYK channels. It should not be captured as "Halftone" data. This is often misunderstood. The halftone capture mode available on many desktop scanners is meant for programs that cannot use grayscale data.

The bit depth or number of levels of information that can be gathered by a scanner is critical to how smoothly a continuous-tone image will reproduce. The maximum number of levels currently reproducible in the PostScript™ output language is 256. To get 256 levels, a scanner must have an 8 bit depth in grayscale and a 24 bit depth for color scanning. See appendix A: Scanning, for more details. These digital levels range from level 255 (0% dot) to 0 (100% dot), white to black respectively.

3. Identify the image category

After an image is scanned, it is helpful to use Photoshop's Histogram feature to display a variety of information about the image. By viewing the histogram, it is possible to tell if the scanner gathered enough levels of data and if the data falls in the proper range. The mean value of the histogram can help determine if the scanned image is in the light, dark, or average image categories.

4. Establish highlights and shadows

To capture and reproduce the critical details in an image, the highlight (lightest) and shadow (darkest) areas must be set to specific target values for individual reproduction requirements. In an image being prepared for printing on offset stock (not newsprint), where the original contains a complete range of tones encompassing both highlight and shadow detail, the digital data should range between levels 240–250 (2–6%) for the lightest areas and between levels 15–5 (95–98%) for the darkest areas. *Normalizing* brings an image in line with these target values. The target values necessary to properly reproduce an image will vary depending on a variety of factors, including the type of paper stock, the specific printing press, and the halftone line screen. When learning about normalized images it is best to discuss the proper target values with your print shop. Basic guidelines for target values are found in appendix B: Calibration.

To normalize an image, the continuous-tone image must be measured either with a densitometer or by comparing it to a known dot % value that would most closely reproduce that continuous-tone shade. This process establishes the relationship of the density (amount of light or dark) of the original image to the

METHODOLOGY

In this section of the book you will get an overview of the key concepts and techniques used in adjusting black-and-white images for reproduction.

STRATEGY

- Examine the original
- Scan the original
- Identify the image category and tones
- Measure and adjust highlights
- Measure and adjust shadows
- Measure and adjust midtones
- Apply Unsharp Mask
- Save file for output or export
- Review image for rescanning or corrections

SAVE THE ORIGINAL SCAN, SAVE THE SETTINGS!

Providing you have enough space on your system, save the original scans and the settings so that after you produce the first proofs, you can go back and make corrections as far back in the process as you would like without starting from scratch.

"D" IS FOR DENSITY

Density is the ability of an object to absorb light. As density increases, less light is reflected

EXPERT INFORMATION

Density values for various media:

Transparency Media
Transparent media is measured in density values that range between 0.0 D to over 4.0 D.
Typical transparency highlights are 0.25 D (+ or - 0.1 D)
Typical transparency shadows are 3.0 D (+ or - 0.25 D)

Reflective Media
Reflective media density values range between 0.0 D to 2.2 D
Typical highlights are 0.05 D (+ or - 0.06 D)
Typical shadows are 1.8 D (+ or - 0.40 D)

Halftone Media
Halftone film media is measured in density 0.05 dmin to 4.0 dmax and dot % values of 0 -100 in 1% increments.
Typical halftone film highlights dot % values are 0-10%
Typical halftone film shadows dot % values are 90-100%

digital values, to the halftone, and to the values printed on paper in the reproduction.

Densitometers are instruments that can measure and display density and % dot values for images. Density is a measure of a reflective original's ability to absorb or reflect light or a transparency's ability to block or transmit light. Densitometers can measure transmissive, reflective, or digital media. They're available in stand-alone desktop and hand-held models, and can be incorporated onto cameras, scanners, and computers. Adobe Photoshop has a built-in digital densitometer. This is the floating Info Palette. It can provide measurements in dot % values or RGB levels.

5. Adjust the midtones

After the end points of an image are chosen, measured, and adjusted, the midtones must be adjusted to achieve the proper separation of tones. The correct amount of midtone adjustment will provide good contrast in the reproduction. Photoshop is optimized for average images and these type of images usually require very little adjustment to their midtones. Light images will require an increase in midtones and dark images will require a decrease in midtones.

If you are not an experienced user and have not done a lot of testing, it is very important that you have calibrated your monitor. The monitor is an important tool in making accurate judgments on midtone adjustments. See page 33 for more information.

6. Sharpen the image

Typically, one of the last adjustments is to add back the sharpness that was lost as a result of the input scanning process. To do this, an Unsharp Mask filter is used. Don't let its name fool you; of all the sharpening features available in Photoshop, Unsharp Mask is the most controllable and is modeled after high-end scanner tools. Some scanners can sharpen on input. Test yours to determine if it produces acceptable results.

7. Save the image

After sharpening, all that is left is to save the image in the correct format and to output an initial round of proofs.

8. Review for corrections

When you get the proofs back, compare the results to the original. If further adjustments are necessary, go back and make them and produce another round of proofs. After some experience you will understand where to go in the process to make corrective adjustments.

EVALUATING AN IMAGE

Printing presses cannot easily print continuous-tone images. To overcome that limitation we create an optical illusion with halftone dots. A screen pattern is used to break the image's continuous tones into various sized dots that give the illusion of shades of gray.

The first step in converting a continuous-tone image to a halftone is to identify the image areas and determine the halftone target values for the reproduction. When the target values are chosen correctly, the reproduction will emulate the original.

SIMULATED PHOTOGRAPH

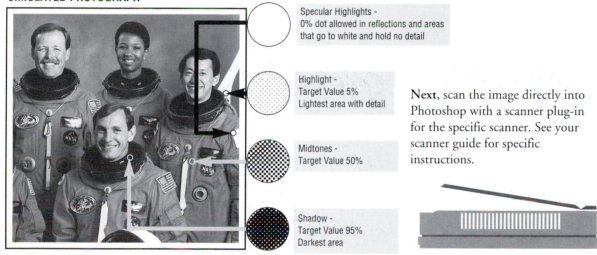

Specular Highlights -
0% dot allowed in reflections and areas that go to white and hold no detail

Highlight -
Target Value 5%
Lightest area with detail

Midtones -
Target Value 50%

Shadow -
Target Value 95%
Darkest area

Next, scan the image directly into Photoshop with a scanner plug-in for the specific scanner. See your scanner guide for specific instructions.

After the image is scanned, the results of the scan can be viewed with the Histogram. For example, the Histogram for this image shows a Mean value of 85. This value helps to identify this image as one that is dark in nature. Also notice that the Histogram is densely packed, indicating that the scanner was indeed gathering 256 levels of data. If it had scanned in 64 levels of gray, three out of every 4 levels would be missing in the histogram.

To view the histogram, select Histogram from the Image menu.

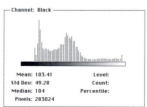

Channel: Black

Mean: 107.80   Level: 107
Std Dev: 48.55   Count: 4701
Median: 115   Percentile: 42.86
Pixels: 658800

Channel: Black

Mean: 103.41   Level:
Std Dev: 49.28   Count:
Median: 104   Percentile:
Pixels: 283024

Histogram of image scan with 256 level grayscale scanner

Histogram of image scan with 64 level grayscale scanner

WARNING! WARNING! WARNING!

If your monitor is not calibrated, you will have to work entirely by using the number display in the Info palette. Failure to do so may result in undesired results. In other words: what you see on screen is not what you get on output. If you would like to learn how to calibrate your monitor for black-and-white work, refer to Appendix B: Calibration.

HOW TO: ADJUST HIGHLIGHTS AND SHADOWS

Adjusting the image to reflect the proper highlight and shadow range is a critical step in achieving a good quality black-and-white image. This process frames the image so that the tonal range can be adjusted to give the best results in reproduction. This is necessary because of the physical limitations of the printing process. For example, an offset printing press cannot hold the detail in images under certain conditions that are specific to each press. If the highlights are too light they may not print. If they are too dark the image may lack contrast. Follow the steps on the next two pages to learn how the highlight and shadow points of an image can be properly identified and adjusted.

WHICH IS MORE CRITICAL TO THE REPRODUCTION: HIGHLIGHT OR SHADOW?

When the highlight dots are off by a few %, the eye perceives a significant amount of change. If a 5% dot is off by 3%, it causes a dramatic change to the highlight, either by loss of highlight detail or by loss of contrast. Shadow placement, though critical, has a larger tolerance. When shadows are off by a few % it is harder for the eye to notice because it is so dark. If a 95% shadow dot is off by 3% it is not as noticeable.

SET HIGHLIGHTS AND SHADOWS

Open a grayscale image file (for this example, it is faster and easier to work on images with a resolution of 72 pixels per inch - see image resampling on page 31). Display the **Info** palette and the **Color Palette** by selecting them from the **Windows** menu.

Preset target values

1. In the first step on page 15, the appropriate target highlight (white point) and shadow (black point) were chosen. The highlight value is 5% and the shadow value is 95%. Compensating for dot gain due to specific printing processes is addressed in the Calibration section.

Input dot 10%
Target: 5% Highlight Dot

Input Dot 100%
Target: 95% Shadow Dot

Determining the proper range of values for the best reproduction is mostly a matter of experience. These values are a good place to start as long as the image actually has highlight and shadow areas.

Tool set-up

2. Use **Levels** to find and set the highlight and shadow points of the grayscale image. Open the Levels dialog box by selecting **Image** and then **Adjust** from the menu bar. Double click on the Set White point (highlight) button. This brings up the Color Picker for the Select White Target Color control. Set the C, M, and Y values to 0 and set the K (black) value to 5%. Click **OK**.

3. Next, double click on the Set Black point (shadow) button in the Levels dialog box. In the Select Black Target Color control, set the C, M, and Y values to 0 and set the K (black) value to 95%.

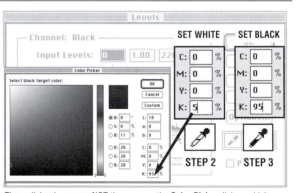

These dialog boxes are NOT the same as the **Color Picker** dialog, which can be selected from the Tool Box. The Set White and Set Black settings are saved to their own locations. The values will remain set from session to session until new values are entered.

Locating the highlight and shadow

4. Determine where the white point or highlight is going to be placed in the image. The Levels tool can help. Click and drag the right hand (white) Input Levels arrow. Hold down the Option key. Slide the arrow to the left and then back right (make sure you have Video LUT Animation checked in the Preferences dialog box and make sure that Preview is not checked). The areas that turn white first are the highlight areas. Return the slider to the full right position. This is a nifty method for quickly identifying the lightest or darkest areas in the image.

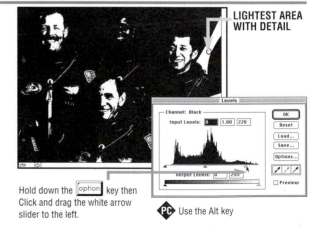

LIGHTEST AREA WITH DETAIL

Hold down the [option] key then Click and drag the white arrow slider to the left.

PC Use the Alt key

5. Now, determine where the black point or shadow is going to be placed. The Levels tool can help. Click and drag the left (black) Input Levels arrow. Hold down the Option key and slide the arrow to the right and then back left. Notice that the image turns black as the triangle is slid right. The first areas that turn black are the shadow areas. Return the slider to the full left position.

PC Use the Alt key

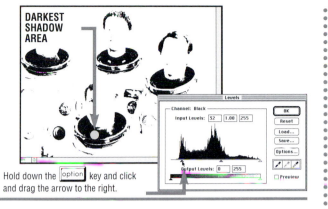

Hold down the option key and click and drag the arrow to the right.

Setting the white and black point

6. To set the white point, click once on the Set White button and then click on the area chosen as the whitest area with detail (the area in step 4). Examine the Info palette setting before choosing the area to set. Confirm the selection by using the eyedropper and measuring the before and after K value in the Info palette densitometer in the area you have chosen as the lightest area with detail.

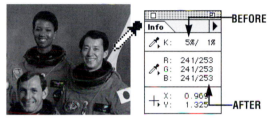

Before and after values are be displayed in the Info box prior to accepting a change.

7. Set the black point by repeating step 6 selecting the Set Black button and choosing the darkest area. This sets the shadow dot. If the adjustments are significant, they will make a dramatic change to the screen image. If they are minor, the change will not be too apparent. Do not close the dialog box! Proceed to the next page.

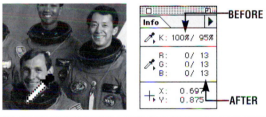

OOPS!

You made the adjustments, but the results are not quite right. This is a subjective decision. Be sure to produce proofs of the images, prior to producing final output. There are two choices to readjust the image:

1. Cancel the dialog box and reopen it.

2. Reset the image to original values by holding down the Option key and clicking Reset (which previously read Cancel), in the dialog box and make the adjustments again.

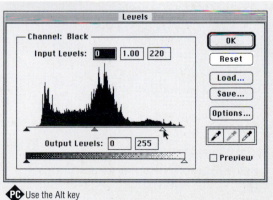

PC Use the Alt key

WHAT IF THERE ISN'T A CLEAR HIGHLIGHT OR SHADOW AREA?

When there isn't an obvious highlight or shadow area, it is not as easy to produce good black-and-white halftones. Even the most experienced operators can take only an educated guess at placing the highlights and shadows in these images. The strategy in this case is to determine a highlight (white) point in the image that will more closely match the original when the image is printed, and apply the value through the Select White Target Color Picker. This might require selecting a white point of 15% K rather than 5%. Use the same strategy if the image does not have a clear shadow area. Use the Select Black Target Color Picker and apply the value that will visually match the original when the image is printed. This might mean setting a black point of 80% black (K) rather than 95%. Experiment with this process to get an idea of how it works.

TARGET VALUE GUIDELINES FOR DIFFERENT IMAGE CHARACTERISTICS:

Average images and images corrected to normal (good balance of light and dark)
Highlight: 5%
Shadow: 95%

High Key (light) or images you want to reproduce light
Highlight: 3-5% less cannot be printed
Shadow: set to the darkest % desired (i.e., an 85% dot)

Low Key (dark) or images you want to reproduce dark
Highlight: set to the lightest % desired (i.e., 20% dot)
Shadow: 95-97% more will likely fill in when printed

HOW TO: ADJUST MIDTONES

After the highlight and shadow areas are established, midtones have to be adjusted. You can make a single point midtone adjustment via the Levels or Curves tool. The Curves tool, however, allows multi-point control over the adjustment of tones between the highlights and shadows. Complex adjustments with Curves are further illustrated in the section **More About Midtones**.

As a rule, light images require an increase in midtones, dark images require a decrease in midtones, and average images require little or no change at all.

GAMMA VALUE TO % DOT CHANGE CONVERSION CHART

GAMMA VALUE								
0.60	0.70	0.80	0.90	1.00	1.10	1.20	1.30	1.40
100	100	100	100	100	100	100	100	100
99	99	98	96	95	94	92	91	89
98	96	95	93	90	88	85	83	81
96	93	91	88	85	82	80	77	75
93	90	87	83	80	77	74	71	68
90	86	83	79	75	72	69	66	63
87	82	78	74	70	67	64	61	58
83	78	73	69	65	62	58	56	53
78	73	68	64	60	56	53	51	48
74	68	64	59	55	52	49	46	44
69	63	58	54	50	47	44	42	39
63	58	53	49	45	42	39	37	35
57	52	47	43	40	37	35	33	31
52	46	42	38	35	33	31	29	27
45	40	36	33	30	28	26	24	23
38	34	30	27	25	23	22	20	19
31	27	24	22	20	18	17	16	15
24	21	19	17	15	14	13	12	11
16	14	13	11	10	9	9	8	7
8	7	6	5	5	5	4	4	4
0	0	0	0	0	0	0	0	0

Read left and right of the 1.0 gamma to calculate how the dot percentages are changed as the gamma is adjusted.

ADJUSTING MIDTONES WITH ONE CONTROL POINT IN LEVELS OR CURVES

1. Determine the correction to the midtones. If your monitor is calibrated, this is a visual and numerical adjustment. See page 33. The example image to the right is a dark image. To optimize this image, the midtones need to be reduced 8-10%. Follow the example below. You can use either the Levels or Curves midtone adjustment. Each tool performs the correction in a different way so results of a similar change are slightly different. You choose which method you prefer.

The mean value of 86.58 indicates that this is a dark image. An 8-10% reduction in midtones would improve this image

Using the Levels midtone (Gamma) adjustment

2. With the dialog box still open and the end points of the image still locked in place, slide the center arrow to the left until the middle input levels box reads 1.3, or type 1.3 in the box. Click **OK**.

If the Levels adjustment is opened again later, you will notice that the endpoint sliders are reset. See the chart on the left sidebar for level adjustment ranges. For this image, a value of 1.3 gamma has been chosen. This selection will result in the 50% dot being shifted to 42%. The highlight and shadow endpoints will not change.

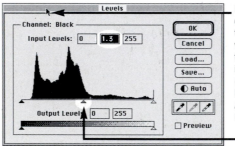

In either the Levels or Curves dialog box, you can click on the title bar of the dialog window to toggle the image to see the before and after image.
(The Preview box must NOT be checked and Video LUT Animation checked in the Preferences: General box.)

Gamma Slider

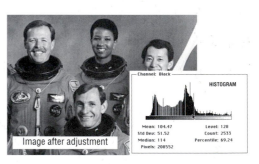

Image after adjustment

Using the Curves midtone adjustment

2. Select **OK** to close the Levels dialog box. Open the Curves dialog box. Move the input and output end points of the curve to 5% (see 1a. in the figure below) and 95% (1b. in the figure below) to prevent them from shifting during a midtone change. The endpoint anchors should match your chosen highlight and shadow values.

3. To make a midtone change with the Curves tool, click the cursor at the 50% point on the curve and pull down on the anchor point keeping the input value at 50%, while moving the output value to 42%. Release the mouse and click **OK**.

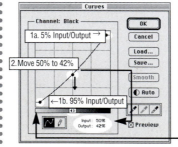

1a. 5% Input/Output →
2. Move 50% to 42%
←1b. 95% Input/Output
Gradation Bar

Be sure the % mode is selected so that the adjustment looks like the Curves dialog to the left. You do this by clicking on the double arrow in the gradation bar.
When in % mode, dragging a point down lightens an image. When working in levels on the curve, dragging a point down darkens an image.

Detail of Gradation Bar

Image after adjustment

UNSHARP MASKING (USM)

This brings us to the final image adjustment to be made prior to saving the file for output: sharpening. When using a scanner, it is often necessary to add sharpness lost during the original scanning process. High-end scanners and some desktop scanners allow the user to add sharpness as the image is being processed. If your scanner supports enhancing sharpness, deactivate this feature for this tutorial.

Refer to the Tools section on page 12 for the details of the Unsharp Mask (USM) adjustment range.

1. With the correct image window active, select Filter: Sharpen: Unsharp Mask from the menu bar.

2. Enter: Amount: 150%; Radius: 1 pixel; Threshold: 0. Click **OK**.

3. To toggle between the before and after effect of the sharpening, use the Edit: Undo command.

Determining the correct amount of sharpness is a subjective decision. If the effect is taken so far that it creates distinct white or black lines in the contrast transition areas of an image, you have over sharpened. Note that the amount of sharpness shown on screen is often softened by the actual printing process, so experiment with various settings.

Image after Highlight, Shadows, and Midtones are adjusted

Image after USM
Amount: 100, Radius: 1, Threshold: 0

Image after USM
Amount: 150, Radius: 1, Threshold: 0

Image after USM
Amount: 200, Radius: 1, Threshold: 0

Image after USM
Amount: 200, Radius: 2, Threshold: 0

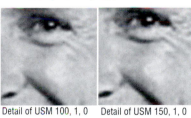
Detail of USM 100, 1, 0   Detail of USM 150, 1, 0

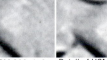
Detail of USM 200, 1, 0   Detail of USM 200, 2, 0

HOW TO:
SHARPEN THE IMAGE

In reproducing images, sharpness "puts the icing on the cake." The strategy is to first adjust the image's highlight, shadow, and midtones to get the best image reproduction, then apply sharpness. If necessary you can go back and make minor image adjustments after sharpness is applied.

LETTING THE SCANNER SHARPEN

An often asked question is, "Should I let my scanner and scanner software make image adjustments or should I do them in Adobe Photoshop?" If you understand how your scanner is performing adjustments such as sharpness and you like them, by all means let the scanner do the adjustments. In a production environment the less user intervention, the better. It is more likely, however, that you will want to use Photoshop at first until you fully understand how the adjustments work. You will then be able to use that experience to evaluate how well the scanner's automatic adjustments are working and you will then understand how to change them manually, if necessary.

HOW TO: SAVE THE FILE

TRANSPARENT WHITES

When a bitmapped file (a file either scanned as line art or converted to a bitmap through the Mode menu) is saved, the EPS dialog box gives you the option to save the image so that the white areas in the image will be completely transparent.

COMPRESSION: LOSSLESS VS LOSSY

LZW compression, named for its developers Lempel, Ziv and Welch, is a lossless form of file compression. It uses magic spells and the tail of a lizard (well, this is better than saying that the compression method uses a mathematical algorithm) to reduce a file's size without losing data. This can save a lot of space if you are sure that the page layout program you are using supports LZW compression. Not all do, so check your page layout program's documentation.

JPEG (Joint Photographic Experts Group) compression is a destructive (lossy) form of file compression that actually throws away data to save space. In Photoshop, the settings range from excellent to fair. The excellent or good settings produce acceptable results and can be used when space becomes an important consideration. Remember, you should compress and recompress images only at the setting used for the first compression. If you keep changing the compression ratio each time you open and close the image, the information degrades quickly. Photoshop's JPEG compression does an excellent job of compressing black-and-white data.

PICT FORMAT

This format should be avoided if at all possible. It is unreliable, corrupts easily, and often causes errors when it is sent to a PostScript™ output device.

SAVE A COPY...

Found under the File menu, this choice allows you to save various stages of the job without replacing the image you are currently working with on screen.

SAVE FORMATS

The primary Save options for black-and-white images created in Adobe Photoshop are **TIFF** (Tagged Image File Format) and **EPS** (Encapsulated PostScript).

TIFF files contain bitmapped data only and should be used if the image will be cropped by the page layout program by a rectangle, circle, or odd shaped box, or if the image will be colored in the page layout program. The image will use the default halftone line screen settings of the page layout program for output. This file format produced smaller files than EPS format and allows the use of LZW (lossless) compression which can save space.

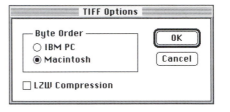

The EPS format in photoshop is a metafile format that contains pixel data and vector data. Vector data allows the user to save the transfer function data, line screen data, clipping path (silhouette) and transparent whites (if the mode has been changed to bitmapped), as part of the file. Line screen and screen angle data saved in this format will override the data in a page layout program.

EPS format supports Mac and TIFF (IBM) bitmap preview options and can encode the file in either binary (which is half the size and takes half the time to download) or ASCII. A note of caution, however: some applications do not currently support binary encoding. In addition, some commercial print spoolers do not support binary encoding. Be sure to check with your service bureau to ensure that they can handle binary files.

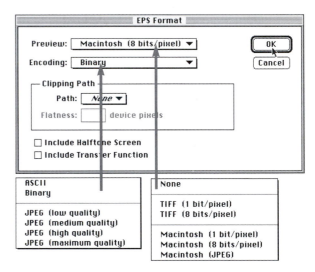

Silhouettes (Clipping Paths)

Clipping paths create a silhouette around an image. To create one, follow these steps:

1. Use the path tool to draw a path around the part of the picture you want silhouetted.
2. Choose Save Path from the Path palette arrow pop-up.
2. Choose Clipping Path from the Paths palette menu.
3. Choose the path from the pop-up choice. You can also choose the path from the EPS save dialog when you go to save the image.

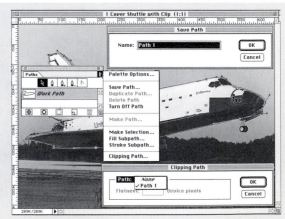

TROUBLESHOOTING BLACK-AND-WHITE HALFTONES

When making corrections based on proofs in a black-and-white image reproduction system, there is a sequence of events that needs to occur to ensure consistent results. This is only possible if a system is in calibration. With a calibrated system, the user can be comfortable knowing there is agreement between each of the system's components. It is then possible to make specific changes, based on proofs, that refine the image reproduction process. The following are typical symptoms and remedies that occur when reproducing black-and-white images.

Symptom: Shadow areas look too dark and lack detail.

Remedy: Measure and check the reproduction's output values. If the shadow values are in agreement with the target values, then correct the reproduction by re-adjusting the shadow areas. Use the Curves tool and decrease the 3/4 tones in 4% or 5% increments until they aren't too dark (see page 8).

If you see more detail in the original continuous tone but can't seem to bring it out with additional adjustments, you might need to re-scan the image.

Symptom: Dark midtones lack detail.

Remedy: If the target value for the shadow is OK and the reproduction is lacking dark midtone detail, reduce the midtones to bring out the detail. Multiple points on Curves technique is useful for this type of adjustment (see page 23). Begin using 5% increments. As more details are identified, finer adjustments will be necessary to finesse the images contrast. If the scanned image data is good this will bring out the important tones of the image. If the scan is poor, then this action will not help. The solution then is to re-scan the image and ensure that enough image detail is captured.

Symptom: Highlight areas lack detail.

Remedy: Measure the highlight areas that are lacking detail. Most likely the highlights are adjusted improperly and do not have enough or any halftone dot areas to carry highlight detail. If the image was scanned without data to carry highlight detail, it requires re-scanning. If the original scan has enough detail but the image processing adjustments were done improperly in the application, then reopen the image and readjust the halftone values, being careful to maintain just enough detail with the new highlight adjustment.

Symptom: The whitest highlight areas have detail but appear "flat," lacking contrast.

Remedy: Measure the highlight areas with the whitest detail. They should be between 1% and 5%. If they are not, then make the necessary adjustments to create enough detail to ensure the image will have enough data to maintain good highlight contrast.

Symptom: Highlight & Shadow areas look and measure OK, but the reproduction lacks overall contrast.

Remedy: If the reproduction looks too light, then increase the midtone. If it is too dark, then reduce the midtone. This increase or decrease will further separate tones creating more contrast. You might try increasing the 3/4 tones and decreasing the 1/4 tones with an S curve, keeping the midtone anchored in place (see page 23 for more curve information).

Symptom: Image lacks sharpness.

Remedy: It is necessary to increase USM. The basic guideline in Photoshop is to use the Amount value and start at 150% (leave the pixel radius at 1 and threshold at 0). Learning to fine tune the amount of USM requires experimentation. It is done by applying different amounts of USM to images, then making film, proofs, and then printing to determine the amount of USM that will provide the correct amount of sharpness.

Symptom: Image appears too sharp.

Remedy: It will be necessary to reduce the sharpness. This technique literally degrades an image. This is done by despeckle, blur, or gaussian blur, until a satisfactory result is achieved. Like sharpness, this is accomplished through experimentation with the appropriate controls.

HOW TO: MAKE CORRECTIONS

GET ORGANIZED

The most successful imaging operations all have one thing in common; every detail of a job's production is organized. When you first start producing black-and-white images, it is important to keep track of your original scan and the saved settings you used to create the final product. The key is to establish a system of folders and file names for storing image files and related information like Curves or Levels parameters (used through Load and Save).

For example, an image management system might consist of 3 folders. One for the original scan, another for final adjusted images, and a third folder for the image adjustment information of Curves and Levels settings. The saved settings can then be used with the original scan as a starting point if additional adjustments need to be made to the corrected image.

Note: You can't save USM settings. Try incorporating them into the file name e.g.,*Scan of President 1,100,0.*

MORE ABOUT MIDTONES

This section discusses the Curves tool and its ability to make a variety of changes that enhance an image's quality.

GEE WHIZ!

Note the diagonal line in the Curves dialog box. As the mouse button is held down over the image, a little round ball appears to visually identify the area that is being probed. This, along with watching the Info palette, will help to locate specific areas of an image on the curve. You can then alter those areas by clicking on the curve in that area and placing a control point. Remember, unless that area is masked, changing that control point will change all the other areas of the image that also have that value.

HOUDINI ACT!

To remove unwanted points on a curve, just drag them outside of the Curves dialog box and they vanish.

WHAT IS CONTRAST?

Contrast is the difference between white and black. If an image has a great difference between the white and black areas, it is identified as having high of contrast. In an extreme sense, the best contrast is in line work where there are only two tones: white and black. On the other end of the spectrum, the worst contrast is a constant level of gray. It can be light or dark gray, but only one level. Understanding these concepts and how they plot on a graph provides us the tools to identify and determine how to create contrast for halftone images using Photoshop.

AVERAGE IMAGES

Because of the way Photoshop was developed, you don't have to introduce many midtone changes for average images, unless something subjective or aesthetic is required in the reproduction. Once the highlight and shadow areas are adjusted properly (based on your experience), the image is ready for sharpening and then printing or export.

The basic moves *(Ensure the highlights and shadows are properly adjusted first)*

There are some basic guidelines for making midtone corrections in images. These corrections are made to optimize the image and compensate for the effects of tone compression that occur when an image is converted from continuous-tone data to digital data and then printed.

Light images (+) midtone

To create contrast in light images, increase the midtone values along the curve at the 50% value. A good starting place is 5%-10 % points from the original position. The only way to trust the results and gain experience is to make and save several incremental changes, produce film and proofs, and compare them to the original and the monitor display.

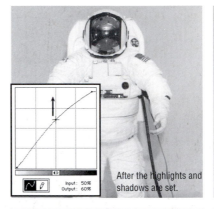
After the highlights and shadows are set.

After increase in midtones.

Dark images (-) midtone

To create contrast in dark images, decrease the midtones. Start with a reduction in midtones between 5%-10% from the 50% input value indicated in the curves dialog box. Make and save several incremental changes and then produce film and proofs and compare them to the monitor display.

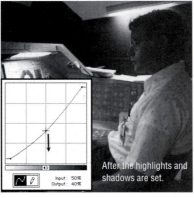
After the highlights and shadows are set.

After decrease in midtones.

Saving settings

After any adjustment is made in Levels or Curves, it is possible to save the parameters of those dialog boxes. This is an easy way to recall the endpoint settings when changing between Levels and Curves. Several sets of different combinations of endpoints can be made and then loaded into the curve prior to making a midtone adjustment. Settings for midtone adjustment can also be saved. Experimenting with and defining your own set of curves will increase your productivity when reproducing multiple halftones.

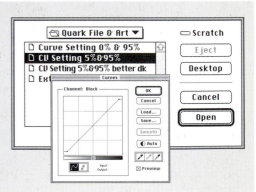

THE MULTI-POINT METHOD FOR MORE DETAILED CONTROL

The multi-point method allows some midtone points to be changed while others are anchored in place and shift only a small amount. This precise control is a delicate balance. If it goes too far in one direction or the other, a trade-off within the reproduction takes place.

Better control with a light image

Increasing the 1/4 tone and the midtones with the multi-point method gives you better contrast in the light image without adversely effecting the 3/4 tone and the shadow areas. The example on the right shows how to use 5 points to create better contrast on a light image.

Better control with a dark image

A dark image, on the other hand, requires a decrease in the 3/4 tone and the midtones to get a better balance between detail and contrast. Remember to anchor the highlight and shadow points on the curve before making curve adjustments.

Better control for average images

An average image can have greater contrast through the use of an "S" curve. This type of curve takes both ends of the tone and separates them, creating more contrast. Be careful not to go too far or the resulting image might appear posterized.

Note: Images on pp. 22 and 23 do not yet have USM applied.

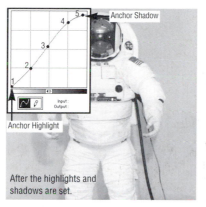

Anchor Shadow

Anchor Highlight

After the highlights and shadows are set.

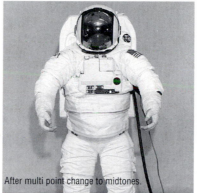

After multi point change to midtones.

After the highlights and shadows are set.

After multi-point change to midtones.

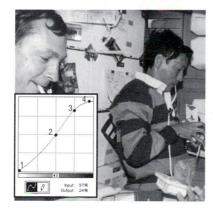

After multi-point change to midtones.

MIDTONE GUIDELINES

The use of one point or multiple points to adjust midtones is dependent on each image's content. The following guidelines outline when to use each method.

One control point

This method works well in situations where images are globally light or dark. Use this method with a dark image where 1/4 tone details are not present or important. In this situation, midtones (1/4 tones-3/4 tones) are reduced globally to bring out the important shadow details.

Multiple points

Use multiple points to bring out details in specific image areas that would otherwise lose them if a global change was made. A multi-point method will permit specific tones to be adjusted while maintaining detail in other areas of the image.

An example of this would be a dark image where important 1/4 tone detail needs to be maintained. In this situation, the 3/4 tone and midtone would be reduced to bring out shadow detail and the 1/4 tone would be anchored in place or increased to differentiate highlight detail.

EXCHANGEABLE CURVES

Curves saved in the Transfer Curves Dialog are fully exchangeable with those saved in the standard Curves dialog. Try the Save and Load functions of both dialogs.

HOW MANY POINTS ARE ENOUGH?

Though it is possible to have up to 16 points to control the reproduction, once 4 or 5 points are understood and adjusted, more points are rarely needed except when creating extraordinary contrast or for special image-correction needs.

CREATING EXTRAORDINARY CONTRAST

ADDING ANCHORS

When adjusting an image using the Curves tool, if areas of the curve start to change in unwanted ways, anchor them in place by adding additional points along the curve.

REFINED GRID IN CURVES

While in the curves dialog box, hold down the Option key and click inside the grid areas to display the 10 x 10 grid.

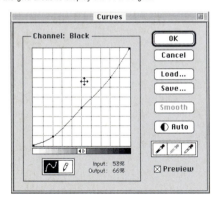

It is possible to use Photoshop's Curves tool to separate tones in specific areas of the image to create extraordinary contrast. You do this by identifying multiple points on the curve and then individually separating areas (moving each closer to a vertical axis) of tones to achieve super contrast. These additional changes are made after completing highlight and shadow adjustments and the basic or multi-point adjustments to the image as described earlier.

1. Open the Curves tool and choose an area where you want more contrast. Use the eyedropper and hold down the mouse button over the point on the image to be adjusted; the Curves dialog displays a small circle on the curve which corresponds to that specific area of the image.

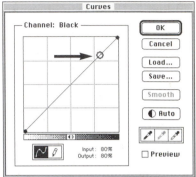

Finding the area you want to separate

2. Move the end points of the curve to your image's white and black points. Anchor parts of the curve that should not change. Now place point (1) on the curve slightly above the selected point and increase it by 2% or 3 %.

3. Next place point (2) on the curve slightly below the selected spot and decrease it by 2% or 3 %. This will increase the contrast.

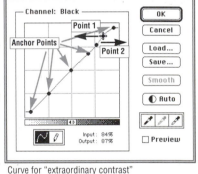

Curve for "extraordinary contrast"

If the points are not too close, this technique will separate the tones and create incredible contrast. Usually, a 2-3% change from the input to output reading is the maximum before posterization starts to show. Practice and testing will show you how far you can go without posterizing the image. As always, film and proofs must be produced and checked against the original image.

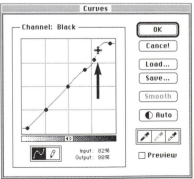

Taking contrast too far

24

Moirés are patterns or "artifacts" that come from rescanning already screened images. Visually a moiré causes noticeable unwanted patterns in the reproduction. Moirés are caused by the overlap of the dot pattern of the original image and the pattern imposed on the image when it is scanned. Moirés should be corrected before applying any sharpening effects. Some scanners have moiré correction as an option. For scanners that don't, try the techniques below.

Base Scan tips

When trying to remove a moiré in an image that will be used at a reduced size i.e., 35%, you will achieve better results if you scan the already screened image at 100% of size, or at 2-3 times the usual resolution. Fix the moiré with one of the techniques below. Then, use Photoshop to resample the image down to the final size.

Gaussian Blur

The Gaussian Blur filter can be applied to an image in varying degrees from .1-100 pixels in strength. A good starting value is 1 pixel. The filter can be applied to the entire image or a mask can be used to apply the effect to only the portion of the image that is most affected by the moiré. Because this effect blurs the image, USM should be used to bring back sharpness.

Despeckle

This technique can be applied alone or in combination with Gaussian Blur. There are no settings for this filter and it does not always sharpen well. While checking the monitor is a good way to evaluate your success, remember to produce film and proofs to confirm your results.

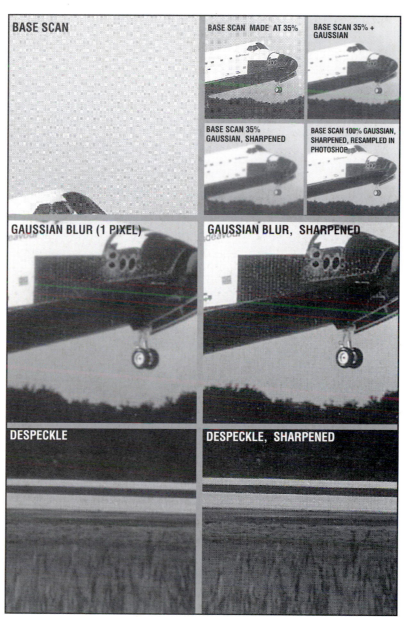

BASE SCAN

BASE SCAN MADE AT 35%

BASE SCAN 35% + GAUSSIAN

BASE SCAN 35% GAUSSIAN, SHARPENED

BASE SCAN 100% GAUSSIAN, SHARPENED, RESAMPLED IN PHOTOSHOP

GAUSSIAN BLUR (1 PIXEL)

GAUSSIAN BLUR, SHARPENED

DESPECKLE

DESPECKLE, SHARPENED

COLOR TO GRAYSCALE

ADVANCED TIP: THE BEST OF TWO CHANNELS

It is possible to blend two channels together to take the best from both to create a new image. If one channel looks pretty good but would be better if you were able to add 50% of another channel to pick up more detail, then try using the Normal Blend setting command found in the Calculations submenu under the Image menu. Experiment with using different amounts of the different image channels that add extra detail. With the preview button checked on you will get to see the results on screen. This technique can be especially helpful with problem images or bad scans.

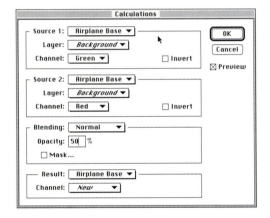

SETTING FOR VIEWING CHANNELS IN BLACK AND WHITE

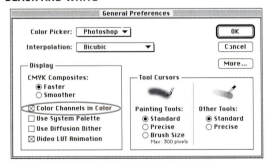

Color Channels in Color should be unchecked.

COLOR IMAGES TO GRAYSCALE

A source image is not often available in black and white. Photoshop provides two primary ways to convert images from color to grayscale.

The standard way to convert an image to grayscale in Photoshop is straightforward:

1. Open the color image file, then go to Mode and select Grayscale.

2. A dialog box will ask if it is OK to discard color information. Click on **OK**. After this image is grayscale it is necessary to set white, black, and midtones using any of the previous techniques.

You can also convert color images to grayscale by deleting two of the three color channels that make up the image. In some cases, this method will produce better results. The distribution of tones within each color channel is based on the image's overall color content. Depending on the image's color make up, one channel might have better contrast than the others, or it might have better contrast than the converted grayscale image.

1. To inspect individual channels in black and white, make sure the Color Channels in Color check box is NOT checked in the General Preferences dialog box.

2. Use ⌘ 1, ⌘ 2, and ⌘ 3 to view each channel. ⌘ Ø permits viewing of the composite color channel.

3. After the best channel is identified, select Grayscale from the Mode menu. The program will keep the selected channel and discard the other two channels.

Finally, set the white and black points and midtones, as described earlier, to achieve the desired halftone results.

PC Use the Control key and 1, 2, 3, or Ø to view the individual channels.

⌘ Ø

⌘ 1

⌘ 2

⌘ 3

GHOSTING METHODS

Photoshop is a full bodied imaging application and offers more than one method to create the same results. This is true when ghosting images. Below are two easy ways to accomplish ghosting.

- Use Levels to reduce the shadow values of an image. This is done with the shadow output levels slider. Move the triangle to the right until the desired amount of ghosting is achieved.

- Use Curves to reduce the shadow values of an image. This is accomplished by adjusting the shadow point of the Curve by reducing the shadow values until the desired amount of ghosting is achieved.

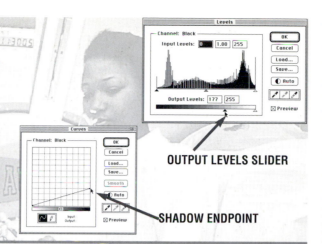

OUTPUT LEVELS SLIDER

SHADOW ENDPOINT

DUST & SCRATCHES

Dust & Scratches is available under the Noise submenu under Filters. It is a great tool for removing minor imperfections quickly. It has a preview window and zoom buttons that help you isolate what you want to view as you apply various values. The Threshold option determines how different the scratch needs to be from the image before the filter is applied. It ranges from 0 to 255, with the strongest effects occurring between 0 and 128. The Radius varies from 1-16 and determines the size of the scratch or spot that will be removed. This filter works well with the use of selection areas before the filter is applied.

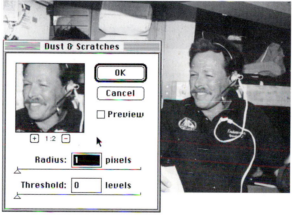

MAKE YOUR OWN CALIBRATION RAMPS

- Make a new file, 8" wide x 1" high.
- Select Grayscale, and 72 DPI.
- Then with the foreground color set to the default 100% black and the background color set to the default white, use the Gradient tool in the tool box to create a ramp like the one you see to the left.

- Then select Image: Map, Posterize from the menu and posterize it 11 levels. The result will be even 10% increments; use 21 levels if you want 5% increments. Now you have a ramp you can send to an output device to check calibration. The value requested in Photoshop should be the value read by a densitometer.

Quick Black & White

Gradient

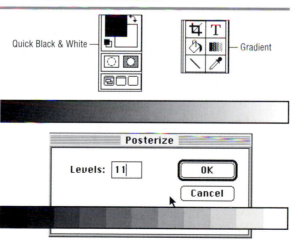

APPENDIX A: SCANNING AND RESAMPLING DATA

SCANNING

Scanning converts original images into digital data for use on a computer workstation. Scanners can be divided into many categories, but for the purposes of this discussion there are two basic categories: high-end and desktop.

High-end scanners - are large, expensive scanners originally manufactured for proprietary (made to work with one system) workstations and have since evolved into input devices for a variety of workstations.

Desktop scanners - are used with desktop computers. They are usually flat-bed scanners but some desktop drum scanners are now available. They are used with Apple Macintosh, IBM/DOS compatible, and many UNIX workstations (Sun, Silicon Graphics, and NeXT, among others).

High-end scanning

High-end scanners are dedicated, high resolution, rotary drum devices, although there are a few flatbed scanners that fit in this category. Rotary drum scanners are identified by their Photo Multiplier Tube (PMT) sensors and flatbed scanners by Charge Coupled Device (CCD) sensors. These scanners have the ability to convert continuous-tone black-and-white and color images into halftone images. These scanners can input both transparent and flexible reflection originals. The input size can vary depending on the model. In some cases, originals over 20" by 24" can be scanned.

These scanners are unique because they provide all the necessary features and functions to produce quality images in one pass. Typically they include high-end features such as converting original images to CMYK, sophisticated tone compression, final scaling and resolution (DPI), screen frequency (LPI) and advanced halftone screening techniques, all in one pass. These features are automatically adjusted and applied during the scanning process. These scanners can directly output final halftone film or they can output an electronic file used with a workstation.

Graphic arts scanners reproduce images well because they were developed specifically to meet print reproduction needs. They are extremely productive, require skilled professionals for their operation, and are expensive.

Desktop scanning

Generating digital images with desktop scanners involves more than the scanner. It consists of a workstation (Macintosh, PC compatible, or UNIX workstation) combined with Photoshop and an imagesetter. The desktop scanner captures grayscale or color digital data that can be adjusted and optimized at the workstation and output with an imagesetter.

When it comes to desktop scanners, there are a wide range of devices available. These devices can vary from extremely low quality to extremely high quality. Desktop scanners are categorized by their sensors, input media features and resolution capabilities. The majority of desktop flatbed scanners use CCD sensors to capture digital data. As desktop computers become more useful for production work, desktop drum scanners are becoming available with PMT sensors. These scanners can offer one or more media input options, including 35mm slides, various size transparencies or reflective originals, and even 3D objects.

Generally desktop scanners have only a few controls, are easy to use, and are available with a variety of resolutions starting around 300 DPI. Once the data from the original is captured by the scanner, it is sent to a workstation for adjustments through software such as Photoshop to optimize the reproduction.

Photoshop is used to adjust and optimize highlight, shadow, and midtone data. These adjustments produce results similar to those created on a graphic arts scanner. After adjustment, the grayscale or halftone file is usually placed into a page layout application on the desktop computer and output to halftone film, via an imagesetter.

Until recently, desktop scanners lagged behind in their ability to produce high quality images. This can be attributed to their evolution from the world of typesetting and design, and not the traditional pre-press environment. As technology advances, desktop scanners and computers equipped with Photoshop are emerging as good production tools and can compete with drum scanners for many types of work. This is especially true for black-and-white images.

GUIDELINES FOR A GOOD DESKTOP SCAN

1. Read the desktop scanner's instructions

Read the manual completely. The instructions convey critical concepts and techniques. For example, some scanners have quick-scan modes. Using this mode can produce extremely fast results, but can provide poorly sampled images. Follow the manufacturer's instructions and guidelines for operating the scanner. Ensure power requirement are met; give the scanner time to warm up.

2. Learn the scanner's mechanics

Each scanner has its own set of image processing functions, such as brightness/contrast, white and black point controls, and gamma. Try and compare the scanner's tools to Photoshop's tools as described in this book. Identify and learn how to use and apply the pre-adjustment controls for functions like previewing, cropping, resolution and image processing. If the instructions for your scanner are vague or unclear, then draw relationships from the Photoshop tools and begin to make assumptions about your scanner controls based on those in Photoshop.

3. Experiment with the scanner's controls

Try scanning a variety of images with the default manual settings or automatic settings. Do one adjustment or function at a time to learn the cause and effect relationships of each tool. If your scanner interface does not have the ability to accept specific values for highlights, shadows, and gamma, then you will most likely need to make these adjustments in Photoshop. Default values can be deceiving and are not always the best values to use for the final scan. Automatic controls often make undesirable adjustments to the image.

During testing, it is necessary to evaluate the results. After the image is scanned, visually and numerically (with the Info palette) check the critical areas to the original to determine if the values will provide a good reproduction. If the results are close, output the image files to an imagesetter and go through a cycle of pre-press proofs. This will provide critical experience and feedback to the operator to determine the cause and effect relationship of the scanning controls, i.e., important details in the highlight, shadow and midtone areas will be seen or not seen. When you understand the scanner controls, the proofs will then allow you to identify what adjustments are required in Photoshop to fine-tune the final image.

4. Identify the scanner's sensors dynamic range, bit depth, and resolution

When black-and-white or color images are scanned, light that represents the image's characteristics (from the lightest to the darkest tones) is reflected or transmitted through filters to the scanner's input sensors. The sensors then convert light into electronic signals that are divided into electronic one and zero bits. The bits are distributed into picture elements or pixels that represent the original image in an electronic form. The number of pixels used to reproduce an image determines the input resolution of the reproduction.

If dynamic range and resolution capabilities of the scanner are not in the scanner's documentation, check with the scanner manufacturer. Find out if the scanner can capture in grayscale and/or color and how many shades it can place in each pixel (you want 256 shades or levels), what density range it can see, its resolution capabilities and the incremental resolution adjustments.

What is dynamic range and how is it measured?

Dynamic range describes the scanner's ability to measure the gradation of tones within a black-and-white or color original. Dynamic range is measured by the range of electronic bits the scanner is

BIT DEPTH AND DISPLAYABLE SHADES/COLORS

1 bit	2^1	= 2 shades black and white
4 bit	2^4	= 64 shades/colors
8 bit	2^8	= 256 shades/colors
24 bit	2^{24}	= 256 shades/colors per channel
		1.68 million colors

HOW MUCH CAN I ENLARGE AN IMAGE ON MY SCANNER?

This chart shows how much a scanner at specific resolutions can enlarge an image and what the resulting dpi will be.

SCALING	Maximum Scanner Resolution		
	300 ppi	600 ppi	1200 ppi
100%	300 ppi	600 ppi	1200 ppi
200%	150 ppi	300 ppi	600 ppi
300%	100 ppi	200 ppi	400 ppi
400%	75 ppi	150 ppi	300 ppi

If you want to be able to make 400% enlargements of an image and still maintain the best DPI:LS ratio for an image that will be reproduced with a 150 line screen, then this chart shows that you will need a 1,200 dpi scanner.

DETERMINING CORRECT SCANNING RESOLUTION

The formula for determining input resolution is:

Input Resolution =
  Quality Factor X Line Screen X % enlargement or Reduction

The chart below shows the results of this calculation for images scanned at 100% of actual size.

Input Resolution / QUALITY FACTOR	Line Screen					
	65 ls	85 ls	100 ls	133 ls	150 ls	200 ls
1:1	65 ppi	85 ppi	100 ppi	133 ppi	150 ppi	200 ppi
1.5:1	97.5 ppi	127.5 ppi	150 ppi	199.5 ppi	225 ppi	300 ppi
1.7:1	110.5 ppi	144.5 ppi	170 ppi	116.1 ppi	255 ppi	340 ppi
2:1	130 ppi	170 ppi	200 ppi	266 ppi	300 ppi	400 ppi

2:1 Best Quality – 1:1 May produce acceptable results. Test first.

capable of capturing (the lightest area minus the darkest area). Transparency scanners used for black-and-white reproduction are capable of capturing a density range between 3.0D to 4.0D. Reflection scanners used for black-and-white reproduction are capable of capturing a density range between 1.5 D to 2.5 D. (The higher the D value, the better.)

What is bit depth?

An 8 bit per pixel scanner has the ability to place 1 of 256 shades (256 levels) of grayscale information in each pixel of information in the resulting grayscale image. For color, an 8 bit scanner can capture 1 of 256 shades (or levels) of red, green, or blue data per pixel. If an image is being scanned with a sensor that has less than 8 bits per pixel, the image will not have enough detail to ensure quality results on high resolution imagesetters.

A scanner with a 4 bit per pixel sensor may produce acceptable results if output to a 300 DPI laser printer or viewed on a monitor. Scanners with 10 or 12 bits per pixel use their greater range to gather more levels of gradation information. When the digital gradations are sampled down or remapped for use in Photoshop, the best 8 bits of data are selected for the image. While these scanners are more expensive, they do provide better quality results. If you want good quality results, a scanner must be capable of capturing a minimum of 8 bits per pixel.

What is resolution?

Scanner resolution is measured by the number of pixels or dots used with different units of measurement, such as inches or millimeters. For example, 300 pixels per inch (PPI), 300 dots per inch (DPI), 12 pixels per millimeter (PPM) refer to the the same resolution. On high-end systems, "Res" numbers are often used. The value Res 12 is equivalent to 304.8 PPI.

What is the relationship between input resolution and halftone line screen?

For an image to be reproduced at a specific quality level, it is necessary to have the correct resolution (or pixels per inch). If not, the image's reproduction will not have enough information to resolve the finer detail of the original. There are guidelines for input resolution and its relationship to the line screen of the halftone output.

Input resolution is identified and measured by the number of pixels (PPI/PPM) or dots (DPI/DPM) in an inch or millimeter. Halftones are identified by the number of lines per inch in the screen used to produce them. In preparing an image for printing to an imagesetter, the number of pixels necessary to achieve a quality reproduction is established based on the halftone line screen. Calculations used to convert pixels into halftone dots show that the best image detail reproduction is achieved when the file contains a 2:1 pixel to line screen ratio. For example, an image scanned at 300 pixels per inch (PPI) is suitable for screening at up to 150 LPI while still maintaining the best quality. To ensure the best reproduction quality, the file needs to contain two pixels for each line screen line. Generally, 1.5 to 1 times the line screen can produce acceptable results depending on your specific project, the printing process, and the type of stock on which you are planning to print. This is especially true if the image is sampled down in Photoshop.

5. Choose the imagesetter resolution and line screen combination that produce 256 levels (shades) of gray

An imagesetter can place a certain number of tiny dots in a square inch area. The number of dots it can place defines its resolution. Imagesetters provide a range of resolutions from 300 to over 3000 DPI. In traditional pre-press work, a range of line screens for halftone reproduction has been established. Typical values are 65, 100, 133, 150, and 200 line screens. The line screen selection will vary based on factors including the paper choice and the type of press. Your print shop can help you choose the correct line screen to meet your project's reproduction needs.

The combination of these two factors, imagesetter resolution, and the halftone line screen, limit the number of possible shades of gray available at a specific imagesetter resolution and line screen value. This relationship is best defined by the use of the following formula:

Gray levels available =

$$\left(\frac{\text{Selected Imagesetter DPI}}{\text{Halftone Line Screen}}\right)^2 + 1$$

If you try different values in this equation, you will discover that lowering the line screen or increasing the imagesetter resolution increases the number of shades of gray. PostScript level 1 currently has a limit of 256 imageable grays. There is no benefit in exceeding 256 steps or shades due to this limit. PostScript Level 2 will allow 12 bit processing resulting in 4096 imageable grays.

6. Scan in the correct mode

Scanners usually have up to four input options: Line Art, Halftone, Grayscale, and Color. To capture the best information for reproducing continuous-tone images, it is necessary to use either Grayscale or Color modes. These modes capture more than 2 bits per pixel and produce shades of gray the imagesetter can convert into appropriate halftone dots.

The Halftone mode is often confusing because it bears the name of the output you are trying to achieve. This function was developed primarily for use in applications that cannot use grayscale data and it does not provide any levels of gray. Do not use this mode when scanning!

7. Periodically scan a reference image

Use a reference image to check scanner parameters. The reference image should be a grayscale or have a variety of detail that will push the envelope of the reproduction system and illustrate visually when all the components of the system are working correctly. If possible, measure the input densities and digital values within the image at common points. Then periodically process the reference image through the entire system. This will establish benchmarks that are easy to check.

8. Provide a good working environment

Environment and work flow

Allow sufficient space for the scanner and for the top to open to position reflective art. Equipment should be arranged so the production operation flows smoothly. Removable media such as floppies and removable hard disks need to be located within reach of the operator. Storage space for floppy disks or other magnetic media must be planned. The ideal situation for scanning would be a totally dirt-free environment. Unfortunately, all environments have some dirt in them. It's important to be aware of positive and negative air flow; positive air flow is the best.

Power protection

Scanners are sensitive to static and fluctuations in the AC power line. Anti-static mats, grounding strips, and surge protectors are useful investments to protect your scanner and computer.

Lighting

Room light should be consistent and easily controlled. Common viewing areas near the scanner should have color correct lighting (5000° Kelvin) for operators to be able to make consistent color judgments.

Cabling

Desktop scanners have a variety of cabling and interface configurations. It is important to double check with the vendor to ensure all the necessary cables are included with the scanner (SCSI or GPIB). If your scanner has a SCSI interface, be sure that the SCSI bus is terminated correctly.

Proofing

Scanning involves producing proofs that are the contracts between the scanning business and the client. It's important to ensure each proof is a quality product. It should be manufactured consistently and without imperfections. This not only keeps customers happy, but permits the scanning operation to avoid costly re-scanning, because of poor judgments.

INTERPOLATION

Each method of interpolation defines the specific calculation that is used to interpolate/create data where none exists. Bicubic is the slowest but produces the best quality. Nearest Neighbor is the fastest but may produce jaggies. Bilinear is between the other two in speed and quality.

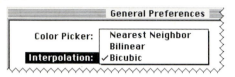

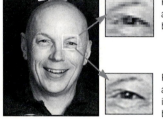

Resized-(scaling) No pixels are added. They just get bigger!

Resampled Up - Pixels added based on Bicubic interpolation. This can only be done in an image editing program.

RESAMPLING AND RESIZING

When scanning images, it is often necessary to change the size of the image after it is scanned so that it fits correctly into your document layout. This involves simple scaling of an image. It often requires that you resample an image, either larger or smaller.

When a digital image is scaled (not resampled), no data is actually thrown away. The process either expands the image size by moving the pixels further apart (reducing the resolution), or it moves the pixels closer together (increasing the resolution). This can be done in Photoshop but it is more often done in a page layout program. While this technique of scaling works, there are several risks associated with it.

The most obvious risk in scaling happens when scaling an image up to a larger size. You may reduce the resolution past the 2:1, 1.5:1, or 1:1 quality factor that you established in your original scan. The result is usually a pixelated image or an image that lacks the detail you expected.

A second, less serious, but not necessarily less costly effect is caused by sizing images down significantly in page layout programs. While the image quality is not adversely affected, the amount of time the image takes to output can be increased significantly. This happens because the RIP (Raster Image Processor) in the printer must calculate the original picture size, calculate the new image size, and then image the picture. (If you want to make it even worse, rotate the image in the picture box.) For one or two pictures, this usually isn't a big problem, but when you have many images, sizing down can add time to producing your project, which can increase costs. The best solution is to go back to Photoshop and apply the proper cropping rotation and image resampling and then reimport the image.

In resampling, an image's data is either created or thrown away. Adobe Photoshop has an excellent built-in tool for just this function, called Image Size. It is available under the Image menu.

If you change the dimensions of the image with the Proportions and File Size boxes checked, the image will be scaled and the image's resolution will be changed. If either dimension is reduced, the resolution is decreased. If you uncheck the File Size box after you have changed to the desired new dimensions, you can then dial in a new resolution. If the new resolution is smaller than the resolution currently shown, then data will be discarded. If the desired resolution is larger than shown, data will be interpolated or created based on the settings chosen in the Interpolation settings in the General Preferences dialog box. See the sidebar on Interpolation for more information.

Photoshop also has an Auto Resolution feature that will determine the correct resolution based on a specified line screen ruling and a quality factor. The Draft quality

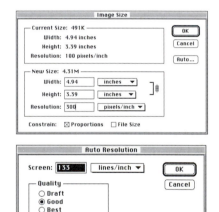

always produces a 72 DPI resolution. The Good quality setting uses a 1.5:1 pixel to line screen ratio and the Best uses a 2:1 ratio. Note that the Screen value is used only for the calculation, you still need to select the correct line screen in the Page Setup dialog box or in your page layout program.

OVERVIEW

Calibration is a complex issue and in the scope of this book can only be addressed in a cursory manner. Specifically, we will comment on the calibration of input scanners and the monitor display. We will also discuss the role of image processing software like Adobe Photoshop and how it affects the output of halftone dots.

Calibration

When a reproduction system is calibrated, all the components in the chain should agree at every stage of the process. Calibration is accomplished by measuring values at various stages of the process. A calibrated system will permit a specific dot value, captured by a scanner, to be measured and adjusted on the workstation, and be output to the imagesetter so the final film will have that exact value. For example, a 50% dot is captured during scanning, confirmed on the workstation, and output to film. The 50% dot value is confirmed by measuring at each stage of the process with digital measuring devices such as a densitometer or Photoshop's Info palette. When each stage numerically agrees, the reproduction system is calibrated.

Key areas to calibrate

Scanner
Monitor
Image processing
Imagesetter
Film chemistry
Platemaking
Printing press

Optimization

Calibration is the basis for optimization. After a system is in calibration, it is then possible to adjust, control and optimize the image values to achieve good reproduction with Photoshop.

For example, a 5% dot value is used to produce a good reproduction of highlight areas. After measuring, it is determined that the original scan was digitized with a 15% highlight dot value. By knowing the system is calibrated, adjustments can be consistently made to reduce the 15% dot to a 5% dot.

The results on the final output film would be the optimum value of a 5% highlight dot. If the system was out of calibration, it would be impossible to achieve predictable and optimized results.

Monitor calibration

To understand monitor calibration, you must learn a variety of skills including how to evaluate images on a monitor, how to use the digital densitometer provided in Photoshop, and the relationship between input scanning and output halftone printing.

If the system has numerical agreement from input to output, but the monitor has not been adjusted to display accurately, the system is not fully calibrated, even though measurements indicate the reproduction is OK. Despite the fact that the numbers agree, the monitor cannot be used to make adjustments because it doesn't visually agree with your output.

Most printers and service bureaus compensate for this lack of full calibration by "working by the numbers." They trust the numbers indicated by the digital densitometer in Photoshop or in their scanner interface and not what they see on the screen display. This method has proven reliable over time but is very difficult for beginners and infrequent operators to use.

Make the effort to calibrate your monitor as well as your system. It'll save you time and money in the long run.

Calibration hardware and software

Monitor calibration can be done with a third party hardware calibrator with custom software, with third party custom software, or with the Gamma control panel provided with Photoshop. One of these should be used, but not all three. Any of these methods will provide system level monitor calibration control. Any other program specific calibration should be deactivated.

CALIBRATION RESPONSIBILITY

Because calibration must occur at all stages along the reproduction process, the responsibility for specific calibration adjustments falls to the person or company in charge of a specific aspect of the reproduction. Due to the altered work flow encountered in the world of desktop publishing, the printer is no longer solely responsible for this issue. If you choose to handle a specific area of the process, you are responsible for the calibration of that area.

CALIBRATE OR BUST?

A properly calibrated system is by far the best environment to work with digital images. However, we live in a world where most people do not have imagesetters or controlled lighting conditions in their working environment. Because of this, it is especially important to learn to "work by the numbers." The operator must learn to use the digital densitometer provided in Photoshop with the Info palette and they must learn to communicate with their service bureaus, so that when they ask for a 5% dot on film they get a 5% dot consistently. In addition, proofing and evaluating is an absolute necessity. *Don't take shortcuts.* Having an uncalibrated system often means that what you see on screen is not what you get on output.

DOT GAIN IN SCREEN TINTS

A note to the prepress savvy: You should also compensate for dot gain in the flat tint screen values you request inside the desktop layout program you use. Most of the dot gain is at the 50% dot and above. Printers usually compensate for this by using pre-compensated screens. Talk to your printer before you select your final screen values so that you agree on how to compensate for dot gain in flat tints.

 In the Windows version, the Calibrate Dialog (AKA Gamma Control Panel) is available through the File menu by selecting the Calibrate button in the Monitor Setup in the Preferences Menu.

The Knoll Gamma Control Panel

The Knoll Gamma Control Panel calibration aid is shipped with Adobe Photoshop. If you did not install it during the installation of the program, the following instructions will explain how to install it and how to use and adjust it for black-and-white image reproduction. If you plan to use the Control Panel to correct your monitor for color work, read through the instructions in the calibration section of the Photoshop manual.

The goal

In a production environment, it would be unwise to trust your monitor as a sole guide to making adjustments. The monitor is an aid in the correction process. A properly calibrated monitor is key when trying to make accurate midtone adjustments. It is very difficult for beginners and occasional users to make midtone adjustments numerically. Try to ensure that the detail you see on screen is the same detail that you will see on the final reproduction. If your expectations are to identify specific dot values on screen, then you will most likely be disappointed with the final printed result.

Important factors

To calibrate the monitor, you must have it set up in a controlled environment and you should know certain information about the monitor.

- The monitor should be placed in a location with consistent lighting conditions (no side lighting from open windows).

- The monitor should be on and warmed up for about 30 minutes before calibration.

- Avoid a bright or busy desktop pattern. It may interfere with your image perception (especially with color images). Neutral gray is best.

Make certain that the Knoll Gamma Control Panel is installed in the Control Panels folder in System 7. Go to the Control Panels folder under the Apple menu (you do have an alias of the Control Panels folder in your Apple menu don't you?) and select the Knoll Gamma Control Panel.

Setting the Knoll Gamma Control Panel

The next few steps are an edited version of the instructions found in your Photoshop manual.

Use the On and Off buttons to turn the Gamma software on and off. If the Control Panel is turned off, the monitor's default values are used.

1. Select the target gamma at the top of the control panel. A setting of 1.8 works well for most images intended for print. Images intended for video should have a gamma of 2.2.

2. Hold up a white piece of paper you wish to match next to the monitor. Click the "White Point" button and drag the red, green, and blue sliders until the monitor white matches the paper color. This corrects for the bluish tint found in most monitor displays (it wouldn't hurt if you could do all this under controlled lighting conditions and 5000° K viewing lights).

3. Standardize the monitor's contrast by dragging the Gamma Adjustment slider until the solid gray areas match the patterned gray areas in the gamma strip above the slider.

4. Adjust the color balance or color cast by selecting the Balance button and dragging the red, green, and blue sliders until the areas in the gray step scale become neutral gray. This compensates for the monitor's color cast.

5. Adjust the black point by clicking on the Black point button and dragging the three sliders until there is no tint in the shadow tones in the gray step scale below the sliders.

6. After you have produced a set of proofs and have a printed piece to compare to, open the Gamma Control Panel again and fine tune your monitor based on how closely the image on screen matches your proof or printed piece. Don't be consumed with making an exact match. Rather, try to get the monitor to reflect the same detail that you are getting on the proof or printed piece. Don't forget, the goal is to have the monitor give you accurate visual cues as to

how well you have adjusted the image. You will still need to measure with the Info palette to determine exact values. Once you have determined the optimum settings in the Gamma Control Panel, save your settings by clicking the Save Settings button. These settings can be reloaded later if you should lose or accidentally change your Gamma settings.

Close the Control Panel when you have finished making adjustments.

Note: Since you have spent much effort in getting your monitor just right, your monitor's adjustments should not be "played with" by you or anyone else using the monitor. Protect those knobs and buttons!

Dot gain

Dot gain is an increase in size of halftone dots from the value that was expected to a larger size. Dot gain in the printing process causes halftone dots to enlarge when printed. In general, most printing processes cause dot gain. The factors that contribute to dot gain include screen ruling, dot shape, printing plates, press blankets, paper, ink, and printing presses. Dot gain will degrade a reproduction especially if the image was not setup to allow for dot gain. The image will usually look too dark.

Build in dot gain

The best way to avoid dot gain problems with the reproduction is to prepare the reproduction with dot gain built in. The customer, the film supplier and printer must communicate and run tests to establish guidelines for each party in the project. Conceptually, the testing involves printing a test form made up of targets and black-and-white reproductions that easily identify the input dot values and the printed dot values. During the test, each stage of the reproduction process is checked and evaluated for the degree of dot gain: digital files, imagesetter film, plating, and the printed dot values. When the amount of dot gain is determined, the black-and-white reproduction can be produced with that amount of gain built in (most printers will know what values you should build in for their presses).

Dot gain and curves

Dot gain is measured by a % dot value and is measured in the midtone regions of the reproduction. For example, if the reproduction system has a 25% dot gain, the 50% dots will print at 75% value. This does not mean all the dot values grow 25%, it means the midtone values gain by 25%. In printing processes, dot gain is thought of in term of curves, with the 50% dot area showing the most gain.

Dot gain can be generated from a variety of sources. The list seems endless. Dot gain can come from variables in the darkroom like fluctuating temperatures of the chemicals in the film processor or film fog, improper pre-press techniques for exposing printing plates, different absorption properties of the papers that are used in printing, or even from the way the printing surfaces of the press are prepared. After dot gain is identified and compensated for in a particular area of the reproduction system, that area can be considered calibrated.

Control dot gain

Once you understand in what area of the process dot gain is occurring, you then need to develop a strategy to control it. You can compensate for dot gain in different places. In the digital world there are no standards established for where in the process to correct for dot gain. Communication with your service bureau/printer is key to achieving the best quality results. Here are some additional guidelines to help you through the process.

1. Some service bureaus/printers routinely adjust customer supplied halftones, some don't. Discuss your project before producing halftones so that you don't double compensate for dot gain.

2. Make sure the imagesetter that you're using for output is calibrated to produce a requested dot value ± 1%.

3. Talk to your printer about the type of press and paper that is being used for printing. Ask the printer to provide you with the amount of dot gain they get on that printing press from film to finished piece.

THE KNOLL GAMMA CONTROL PANEL

This tool allows the user to save and load settings for different uses. These settings can be used to standardize all the monitors in a given location so that information from a given job looks the same on each machine. If you are going to do this often, it is probably worthwhile to get a hardware screen calibration device.

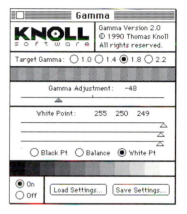

 In the Windows version, Gamma control is available through the Calibrate button in the Monitor Setup in the Preferences menu in the File menu.

DOT GAIN FACTOR RELATIONSHIPS TO HALFTONE TARGET VALUES

Printing Press	Paper Stock	Line Screen Ruling	Highlight Dot	Shadow Dot	Dot * Shape
Sheetfed	Newsprint	85-120	3-5	85-90	Round
	Uncoated	100-150	3-7	90-95	Round
	Coated	133-200+	3-7	90-98	Round
Web	Newsprint	65-120	1-3	75-90	Round
	Uncoated	100-133	3-7	85-95	Round
	Coated	133-200+	3-7	90-98	Round

*Round dots have proven to display the least amount of dot gain. Square dots provide sharper results. Ellipitical dots create smoother flesh tones and less banding. *Postscript Screening*, Peter Fink

4. Learn about the relationship of line screen ruling to printing stock and press and how it controls dot gain. See the side bar on the left for guidelines.

There are variety of options to compensate for dot gain. Each image reproduction should develop consistent guidelines for compensation for the dot gain.

The most often used option is to adjust the scanned original to produce what you believe to be good highlight, shadow and midtone values based on the printers dot gain specifications. If you use this method, it is important to have proofs produced that accurately show how the image will print with the dot gain added back in. When the correct information is provided, this method should provide good results for a given paper and press condition at the specified amount of dot gain. As a guideline, you can produce the image so that it looks good on a non-compensated proof, and then reduce the midtone curve of the image to compensate for the printer's specified dot gain.

More about dot gain

Typically, highlight dots appear to gain very little, if at all, in a sheetfed printing process. In web printing, especially on newsprint, highlight dots can gain over 5%.

Imagine a printing process that was determined to have a 30% dot gain overall. To reproduce the image correctly, it would be necessary to identify the amount of dot gain from each area of the reproduction process then compensate for this gain during the image processing stage. i.e., make the proper adjustments in Photoshop for highlight, midtone and shadow placement. Typically in a process where the highlight gains 3%, a 2% target dot value would be compensated for in the halftone film. So when printed, it would reproduce as a 5% dot.

Conversely, if the shadow areas gained 10%, the shadow dots would be created with an 85% target dot value. So when printed it would reproduce as a 95% dot. This example illustrates that by anticipating dot gain in the printing process, it is possible to compensate in the highlights, shadows and midtones of an image to achieve a good reproduction.

System setup

Establishing any type of image reproduction system is not a quick process. Some businesses expect instant results because they have a lot of money and time invested. To establish a black-and-white image reproduction system, equipment needs to be installed and calibrated, bugs need to be worked out, personnel need to be trained, a work-flow system needs to be established, ancillary systems like proofing must be established, customer requirements must be defined, then the product has to be produced. This process typically takes from one to six months.

Scanner setup

Scanner setup can be a difficult and technical process. A lot of time and frustration can be saved if you utilize vendor support or seek out a qualified pre-press professional. If the critical areas of the reproduction are not correct after scanning, they need to be adjusted either through the scanner software or through Photoshop.

The most productive strategy is to establish average setup parameters that allow the scanner to provide the best data with minimal adjustments through Photoshop. However, depending on the scanner interface, this is not always possible.

Test the system

To calibrate a system, testing is necessary to determine what adjustments need to be made. A good starting point is to acquire a grayscale step wedge from the scanner vendor, a graphic arts dealer or from a photographic supply house. With this method, you scan a grayscale into the desktop workstation. Use the eyedropper and the Info palette in Photoshop to measure the the whitest and darkest step on the grayscale. For example, when setting up your system, if the scan of the grayscale measures a 10% dot in the area of the scale that you have determined should contain no dot, then adjustments need to be made to cause the correct value to appear where you expect to see it. The specific input scan correction will depend on the software for each desktop scanner.

Start by adjusting scanner controls to determine if they can change the highlight or shadow point of the scan without degrading the overall results. If the correct highlight is achieved, but the rest of the image is too light, then it might not be possible to use the scanner's controls to normalize the image, and you will need to use Photoshop to do the job. If this is the case, the goal in scanning is to find the settings that capture the best image detail and balance of tones. Then use Photoshop to finish the process.

After the scanner controls are adjusted so the grayscale has the best data the scanner can capture, use Photoshop to measure and adjust the highlight and shadow areas to the target values. The goal is to establish the setting of the scanner and Photoshop to closely match the grayscale. Making proofs is critical to determining your success in this process.

Run multiple tests

This process will take a number of iterations of film and proofs. After the grayscale or standard guide looks acceptable, several average images will be reproduced with the average setup data. If this testing is done in Photoshop, only the highlight and shadow should require adjustment, because Photoshop is designed to correctly establish the midtone on an average image without additional user intervention. After a number of average originals are scanned, adjusted, proofed and evaluated, a trend will emerge to illustrate the good and bad characteristics of the average setup. Once these trends are identified, corrective action is necessary to correct for any negative results of the initial average setup data. This is done until the program is fine tuned, making it possible to produce average images without

major problems. Testing and proofing should also be done with several light and dark images. This will establish the correct midtone adjustment ranges for these images.

GLOSSARY

Analog — Description of the continuous wave or signal (such as the human voice) using an electrical voltage variation. Used for voice, visual, and computer data communication. The digital or pulse output of a computer or terminal must be converted to an analog signal before it can be transmitted over analog-grade lines.

Anamorphic Sizing — Unequal scale change in the horizontal and vertical direction of a scanner. This enables the scanner to adjust the ratio in the horizontal and vertical direction.

Artifact — A visible indication (defect) in an image, caused by limitations in the reproduction process.

ASCII — (American Standard Code for Information Interchange) Standard by which many computers assign code numbers to letters, numbers and symbols. Used for text exchange between computer platforms.

Banding — A visible stair-stepping of shades in a gradient.

Binary — Numbering system having only two values, 0 and 1. Base 2 numbering scheme.

Bit — The smallest unit of information in a computer. It can define, by itself, one of two conditions (on or off).

Bit-Map — An image formed by rectangular grid of picture elements (pixels). The computer assigns a value to each pixel, from one bit of information (to indicate black or white), to 24 bits per pixel for full-color computer displays, to as much as 64 bits per pixel for some types of full-color images.

Brightness — The intensity of a color or tone regardless of its hue or saturation.

Byte — Basic unit of information in a computer. Consists of a sequence of eight binary bits, usually handled as a unit. One byte usually represents one character.

Calibration — Setting equipment to a standard measure to produce reliable results.

CCD — (Charge Coupled Device) A diode that is light-sensitive when charged with electrical voltage.

Clipping — Process of setting graphics display boundaries. The clipping volume is defined by the window, near and far clipping planes, and projectors of the corners of the window. Data on the planes forming the edges are considered to be within the volume.

Color Space — Three-dimensional model (or representation of a 3D model) used to organize colors to show progressions of hue, lightness, and saturation. Device-independent color spaces are based on international standards (CIE).

Continuous-Tone Copy — Image that has a complete range of tones from black to white: photographs, paintings and drawings. Negative or positive with a broad range of tones that have no screened dots.

Chromalin™ — An off-press color proofing system developed by DuPont. The proofs are single laminated sheets produced from film separations.

CT (Continuous tone). — A file format used for exchanging high-level scanned information.

Data Compression — "Squeezing" of data for the purpose of transmission throughput or storage efficiency. Portions of the data are removed using an algorithm that will restore the data when needed.

Default — Command or parameter that takes effect if no other option is specified.

Density — The ability of a material to absorb light. Measure of the light-transmission of a transparent or translucent object or the light-absorbency of a reflective surface. In photography, measurement of the opacity of a transparent or translucent object. On a film negative, the greater the density area, the more black or more developed it is. Density is measured from 0 to 4.0. It is calculated by measuring the reflectance or transmittance of light and calculating theoretical light absorption.

Densitometry — A method of measuring tonal value based on the light absorbing properties of grays or colorants. Densitometers are used to measure the transmission of reflection of samples through selected blue, green, red, and visual filters.

Digital — Method of data storage and/or transmission wherein each element of information is given a unique combination of numerical values (bits). Each bit indicates either the presence or absence of a condition (such as on-off, yes-no, true-false, open-closed). Modems convert the pulsating digital signals into analog waves for transmission over conventional telephone lines.

Digital-to-Analog Conversion (D/A) — Conversion of digital information into a state of fluctuating voltage levels. (DAC) Interface to convert digital data (represented in discrete, discontinuous form) into analog data (represented in continuous form).

Direct-Digital Color Proof — A proof made from a stored data file onto a substrate without producing intermediate separation film.

Display — Temporary visual representation of computer output on a CRT or other electronic device.

Dmax — The highest level of density of a film positive or negative.

Dot — Smallest visible point that can be displayed on a display surface.

Dot Gain — The increase in halftone dot values that occur during the offset printing production process. Total dot gain is measured as the difference in apparent dot size between the final printed product and the original film. Dot gain occurs as the result of both mechanical and optical influences on the original dot size.

Dots, Halftone — Minute, symmetrical individual subdivisions of the printing surface formed by a half-tone screen.

DPI (Dots-Per-Inch) — A method of denoting the resolution of a scanned image, a digitized image in a file, or an image as rendered by an output device. Also, used interchangeably with pixels per inch (PPI).

Drum Scanner — An optical input device that mounts reflective or transparent input media on a revolving cylinder for digitizing.

EPS — Encapsulated PostScript, this format carries a pict preview and is the only format that supports saving line screen data and transfer functions. In bitmapped mode, it also supports transparent whites.

Export — To output data in a form that another program can read.

File — A named collection of information stored as an apparent unit on a secondary storage medium such as a disk drive.

Film — Photosensitive material, generally on a transparent base, which will receive character images, and may be chemically processed to expose those images. In imagesetting, any photosensitive material, transparent or not, may be called film.

Flat-bed Scanner — An optical input device that mounts the image on a flat plane rather than a revolving cylinder.

Gamma — The measure of compression or expansion of the shades of colors in an image. Gamma correction compresses or expands the range of tones in each hue.

Gamut — The range of hues that can be reproduced from a given technology, process, and set of colorants in all combinations.

Gigabyte — A unit of measure of stored data corresponding to one billion bytes of information.

Gradation (contrast) — A relationship of the distribution of tone values in the reproduction to the original.

Graphics — Term used to refer to any presentation or generation of information in visual form.

Gray Scale — An orderly variable progression in definite steps of gray densities ranging from minimum zero (white) to maximum density (black). A strip of standard gray tones placed at the side of the original copy during a photography to measure tonal range obtained. Used in processing film or materials such as photographic paper and plates.

Grayscale — The depiction of gray tone between black and white.

Halftone — an image created with a pattern of data for different sizes used to simulate a continuous-tone photograph, either in color or black and white. The halftone screen converts continuous-tone copy to line copy (discrete dots of varying sizes and shapes) for printing on press.

Hard Disk — Non-flexible disk that can hold much more data than a floppy disk. Hark disk storage is measured in megabytes. It is more expensive than a diskette, but is capable of storing much more data.

High Contrast — Reproduction technique in photography with high gamma in which the difference in darkness (density) between neighboring areas is greater than in the original.

High Key — A very light original image (possibly overexposed) that contains important detail in the highlight area.

Highlight — The lightest or whitest part of an image with discernible detail. A highlight is represented in a halftone image by the smallest dot patterns. A specular highlight is whiter and lighter, but has no detail.

Histogram — A graphic representation of the number of pixels with given color values, showing the breakdown or distribution of color values in a picture.

Imagesetter — Device that sets type, graphics and half-tone imagery using digital lasers outputting at high-resolution to photosensitive material or plain paper.

Input — Raw data, text, graphics, imagery or commands inserted into a computer.

Input/Output (I/O) — Term for the equipment used to communicate with a computer system. Examples of I/O devices are: a keyboard, a mouse, a floppy disc drive, or a printer.

JPEG — (Joint Photographic Expert Group) An image compression/decompression standard that divides the image area into cells to condense information based on content analysis.

K — (1) Abbreviation for the color black. K is used so that it is not confused with an abbreviation for the color blue. (2) Represents "kilobytes" of information which is 1024 bits. The K is upper-case to distinguish it from lower-case k, which is a standard international unit for "kilo," or 1,000.

Laser Printer — Computer output device that uses a laser to generate the character image. It uses some of the same methods to produce the final image as a copier.

Lossy — Data compression algorithms that assumes some of the data in an image file is unnecessary and can be eliminated without affecting the perceived image quality. Typically this type of compression has ratios between 10:1 and 100:1.

Lossless — Data compression algorithms that store data in a more efficient format that does not cause any data loss in the compression process. Typically this type of compression has a ratio of up to 8:1.

Low Key — A dark image (possibly underexposed) that contains important detail in the shadow area.

LPI (Lines Per Inch) — A measure of the frequency of a halftone screen.

LUT (Look Up Table) – A method of converting from one color space (color representation) into another, either to compress the source color gamut or to map specified colors into the available gamut of an output device such as a display, printer, or film recorder. Also, the table of colors that a computer can display at a given time.

Megabyte (Mbytes) — A unit of measure of stored data corresponding to a million bytes of information. (Actually 1,048,576 bytes of computer storage.)

Memory — A device into which data can be entered, in which it can be held, and from which is can be retrieved at a later time. Data is stored in digitally encoded bits, and manipulated as needed during calculation processes. The amount of memory a computer has directly affects its ability to perform complex functions.

Midtones — Tonal values located between highlights and shadows. Midtone placement controls contrast of the reproduction by determining the separation of tones in an image.

Moiré — Undesirable screen pattern in color process printing caused by incorrect screen angles of halftones.

Monitor — Electronic display unit that uses cathode ray tube to generate text, graphics and imagery. It looks like a normal TV set, however, the monitor has a much higher degree of resolution.

Monitor Calibration — The process of optimizing the color settings of a monitor to match selected colors of a printed output.

Monotone or Monochrome — Artwork reproduced in one color only. Also black-and-white copy.

Neutral Gray — Any level of optical density (from white to black) having no apparent hue. It consists of equal levels of red, green, and blue (RGB).

Offset Lithography — Commercial form of lithographic printing. Offset lithography is a planographic printing method; it is the only major printing method in which the image area and the non-image area of the printing plate are on the same plane. They are separated by chemical means, on the principle that grease (ink) and water (the etch in the fountain solution) do not mix. The ink is transferred from the plate onto a rubber blanket and then to the paper.

Off-Press Proof — A color proof generated prior to the production press run and prior to, or in lieu of, a press proof.

Output — Process of sending computer results to a CRT or printer.

Photomultiplier Tube (PMT) — A light sensitive tube that can detect very low light levels by amplifying the signals applied to it. Usually associated with drum scanners.

PICT/PICT2 — The Apple Macintosh format for defining bitmapped or object-oriented images. The more recent format PICT2 supports 24 bit color.

Pixel — An acronym for Picture element; minimum raster display element, represented as a point with a specified color or intensity level. A two-dimensional array of dots that define the form and color of an image. Measurement is indicated as PPI (pixels per inch).

Posterize — The accidental or intentional effect of reducing the number of shades in an image between the lightest and darkest shades.

PostScript™ — The standard device-independent language developed by Adobe Systems that describes the appearance of pages in documents. PostScript describes a page in its final form, ready for imaging on an output device. Encapsulated PostScript describes a graphic, image or complete page in a final form in a way that can be exchanged between application programs so that one PostScript described item can be included in another layout.

PPI (Pixels Per Inch) — A measure of the amount of scanned information. The finer the optics of the scanner the higher the scan resolution. PPI is equivalent to DPI.

Prepress Proof — Proof made before the final press run by exposing the film negatives or positives to pigmented or dyed light sensitive materials. When assembled, it will be similar in appearance to the finished printed product.

Prescan — A preliminary or preview scan of an original to determine the correct setup and cropping prior to full scanning.

Printing Plate — Surface, usually made of metal, that has been treated to carry an image. The plate is inked and the ink is transferred to the paper or other surfaces by a printing press. Printing plates are also made of rubber, synthetic rubber, and plastics.

Proof — Working copy of some material used for review and approval. A reasonably accurate sample of how a finished piece is intended to look.

RAM (Random Access Memory) — Volatile memory that can be written to or read from by a program, and in which the memory locations can be accessed in a random sequence. RAM may be expanded by adding memory chips or memory boards.

Random Proof — A proof consisting of many images ganged on one substrate and positioned with no regard to final page imposition.

Raster — The series of lines of information such as the parallel horizontal scan lines that form a television or video display image.

Reflective Art — Items that are reproduced using light reflected from their surface.

Resolution — The measure of image details. The smallest discernible detail in visual rendering. Resolution may be stated in terms of spot diameter, line width, pixel matrix dimension, raster lines or dots/inch.

RES — Unit of measure of resolution in number of lines per millimeter, such as RES8 or RES100. To convert RES to DPI, multiply the RES value by the number of millimeters in an inch, 25.4 (for example, RES12 = 300 DPI).

Retouching — Art of making digital, chemical, or dye corrections by adding or removing density or color, on continuous-tone film, on color transparency materials or on reflection prints. Digital retouching makes changes to pixel values to enhance image appearance.

RGB (Red, green and blue) — A color space that represents colors as an additive mixture of red, green and blue light.

RIP (Raster Image Processor) — Part of an output device that rasterizes, or converts mathematical and digital information into a series of dots, so that it can be rendered and imaged onto a screen, film, paper or other media.

Scale — To change the proportion of an image by increasing or decreasing its size.

Scan — To examine or capture an image by means of a moving light beam or "flying spot." Scanning technology is used in imaging, optical character recognition, as well as in other areas.

Scanner — Electronic input device that converts art or continuous-tone images into digital form. Digital scanners convert line art (black-and-white), monochrome images (gray levels), and full-color images into pixel arrays. Some scanners are also color separation machines that use circuits to color correct, compress the tones, and enhance detail.

Screen — To break up continuous-tone copy into dots for reproduction as a halftone. Line screens are designated by the number of ruled lines they contain: from 50 lines per inch to 500 lines per inch. The greater the number of lines per inch, the sharper and fine the printed half-tone. The selection of the screen is dictated by the paper, press, the nature of the copy.

Screen Ruling or Frequency — The number of lines per inch in the halftone screen. The lower the number, the larger and more widely spaced the dots. Higher screen rulings allow reproduction of fine detail.

Service Bureau — A business that specializes in outputting computer files on laser imagesetters, film recorders, large-format plotters and other types of output devices.

Shadow — The darkest part of an image with discernible details, represented in halftone images by the largest dot patterns.

Sharpen — Electronic photo-retouching function for enhancing image detail and contrast either globally or in selected regions of the picture.

Sheet-Fed — Press configuration where the paper is fed into the press as sheets rather than a web.

Specular Highlight — Small reflection or detail highlight in a photograph that is reproduced in halftone form with a 0% dot value.

Spot — Smallest region of an input or output image whose tone can be controlled independently of all other regions. A digitally generated halftone dot is constructed using a matrix of spots.

TIFF (Tagged Image File Format) — A file format developed by Aldus Corporation for exchanging bitmapped, monochrome, and full-color images between applications.

Tone Compression — A reduction in the range of the hues and values in an original.

Transparency — A positive photograph on transparent film such as Agfachrome, Kodachrome, or Ektachrome™ film, usable as copy for color separation and viewed by transmitted light. A positive color image of the original drawing, painting or scene on a colored photographic film is also referred to as a chrome.

Transparency Scanner — An optical input system for digitizing images from small format positive or negative transparency film.

USM (Unsharp Masking) — The term comes from a conventional color separation camera technique that uses a unsharp photographic mask to increase contrast between light and dark areas of the reproduction and gives the illusion of sharpness.

BIBLIOGRAPHY

Adobe Systems Incorporated
*Adobe Photoshop User Guide Version 2.5
for Macintosh,*
 Mountain View, CA
1993

Adobe Systems Incorporated
*Adobe Photoshop User Guide Version 3
for Macintosh,*
 Mountain View, CA
1994

Beale, Stephen and Cavuoto, James
The Scanner Book
Micro Press
Torrance, CA
1989

Busch, David D.
*The Complete Scanner Toolkit
Macintosh Edition*
Business One Irwin
Homewood, Il
1992

Bruno, Michael H.
Principles of Color Proofing,
Gamma Communications
Salem, NH
1986

Campbell, Alastair
The Mac Designer's Handbook
Running Press
Philadelphia, PA
1992

Fink, Peter
PostScript™ Screening Technology
Adobe Press
Mountain View, CA
1992

Hannaford, Steve
An Introduction to Digital Prepress
AGFA Corporation
Wilmington, MA
1990

Lawler, Brian P.
What Makes a Good Halftone?
Self Published (805) 544-8814
San Luis Obispo, CA
1992

Molla, R. K.
Electronic Color Separation
R.K. Printing & Publishing Company
Montgomery, WV
1988

Murry, James D. and William vanRyper
Graphic File Formats
O'Reilly & Associates, Inc.
Sebastopol, CA
1994

Roth, Steve
"Halftones Demystified" Macworld
February, 1993 pp. 175-180
Ziff Communications Company
1993

Rich, Jim
Evaluating High Performance Color Scanners
Rich & Associates
Olney, MD
1993

Rich, Jim
The Macintosh Pre-Press Workshop series
Rich & Associates
Olney, MD
1991

Sakhuja, Sanjay
Digital Color Prepress Volume Two
AGFA Corporation
Wilmington, MA
1990

Southworth, Miles
Color Separation Techniques
Graphic Arts Publishing Co.
Livonia, NY
1979

Southworth, Miles
Pocket Guide to Color Reproduction
Graphic Arts Publishing Co
Livonia, NY
1979

Related Peachpit Titles

4 Colors/One Image
Mattias Nyman
Peachpit Press
1993

Photoshop 2.5 for Windows: Visual QuickStart Guide
Elaine Weinmann and Peter Lourekas
Peachpit Press
1993

Photoshop 3 for Macintosh: Visual QuickStart Guide
Elaine Weinmann and Peter Lourekas
Peachpit Press
1995

The Photoshop Wow! Book
Linnea Dayton and Jack Davis
Peachpit Press
1993

Real World Scanning and Halftones
Stephen Roth and David Blatner
Peachpit Press
1993

Understanding Desktop Color
Michael Kieran
Peachpit Press
1994

INDEX

INDEX

INDEX

ABOUT THE AUTHORS

Sandy Bozek – brings a unique combination of technical skills, graphics arts management experience, and financial analysis capabilities to clients in the printing and publishing industries.

After graduating with a degree in Industrial Training, from Old Dominion University, Sandy began her career as an offset stripper, at French Bray Printing, a quality half-web and sheet-fed printer in the Baltimore/Washington area. There she managed the company's first electronic pre-press equipment. She worked closely with clients and the sales staff to further their understanding of the capabilities of the new equipment, and later moved into sales.

She left printing sales to become the production manager at the Adams Group, an Advertising firm in Rockville Maryland. In 1989 she was hired by Credit Card Service Corporation, a national direct mail marketing firm in Springfield, Virginia, to become Director of Production. There she managed creative and production services for collateral work and new product development.

In 1991, Sandy launched Bozek Desktop Inc., a desktop publishing management consultancy, specializing in project management, systems integration, and training, for design, printing and publishing environments. Her clients include: Baltimore Gas & Electric Company, the Australia America Association, the Recording Institute of America as well as prepress trade shops and printing companies.

In addition to belonging to various electronic publishing and pre-press users groups, Sandy teaches courses for Montgomery College, Anne Arundel County Continuing Education, Maryland Institute of Art, and the Printing Industries of Maryland.

Jim Rich – is president of Rich & Associates a Washington D.C. area consulting firm that specializes in pre-press training, hands on workshops, leading edge research, publishing and college level curriculum development. He brings a perspective of twenty years experience of hands on applications, research and consulting with black and white and color methods in the graphic arts and emerging desktop imaging markets.

Jim has been affiliated with imaging businesses that include companies such as Adobe Systems Inc., The Center for Creative Imaging, Crosfield Electronics, Electronics for Imaging, The Lanman Companies, The National Geographic Society, Miles / AGFA, various trade shops and service bureaus.

His responsibilities have encompassed selecting black and white and color scanning and page layout systems as well as installation, research and development, production management, course development and pre-press training programs.

Jim developed the Macintosh Pre-Press Workshop Series. These courses are a mix of hour long, half day, one day, two day and extended learning programs. The workshops combine lectures and hands-on instruction to provide students with a complete review of black and white and color pre-press techniques, and calibration methods. Each participant is provided hard to find black and white and color imaging information, unique reference materials and the opportunity to learn practical black and white and color reproduction skills

Mr. Rich holds a Masters degrees from the Rochester Institute of Technology in the Printing Technology.

More from Peachpit Press...

Four Colors/One Image
Mattias Nyman

This practical, full-color book provides background information as well as procedures for reproducing and manipulating color images using Photoshop, QuarkXPress, and Cachet. *$18.00 (96 pages)*

Illustrator 5.0/5.5 for Macintosh: Visual QuickStart Guide
Elaine Weinmann and Peter Lourekas

Written in the same style as Elaine Weinmann's award-winning, best-selling QuarkXPress Visual QuickStart Guide, this indispensable step-by-step guide covers the basics of Illustrator and the latest features of Illustrator 5.5. *$17.95 (240 pages)*

The Little Online Book
Alfred Glossbrenner

A beginner's guide to everything you need to begin exploring the electronic universe from your desktop. Covers modems, the Internet, and online services. Also includes a step-by-step cookbook explaining common online tasks. *$17.95 (380 pages)*

The Mac is not a typewriter
Robin Williams

Covers the top twenty things you need to know to make your documents look clean and professional, including em dashes, curly quotes, spaces, indents, white space, and more. *$9.95 (72 pages)*

The Macintosh Bible, 5th Edition
Edited by Darcy DiNucci

Now completely updated, this classic is crammed with tips, tricks, and shortcuts that cover the most current software and hardware. New chapters highlight multimedia, children's software, PowerPCs, and more. *$30.00 (1,170 pages)*

The Non-Designer's Design Book
Robin Williams

This book is for anyone who needs to design, but who has no background or formal training in the field. Follow these basic principles and your work will look more professional. Full of design exercises and quizzes. *$14.95 (144 pages)*

Peachpit's PageMaker 5 Companion
Robin Williams
with Vicki Calkins and Barbara Sikora

Find out why this innovative, comprehensive reference book is a "must-have" for both novice and experienced desktop publishers. You'll discover quick and concise answers to any PageMaker question with numerous sidebars, quotes, and real-life wisdom from bestselling author Robin Williams. *$34.95 (964 pages)*

Photoshop 3: Visual QuickStart Guide
Elaine Weinmann and Peter Lourekas

The author of our award-winning *QuarkXPress 3.2: Visual QuickStart Guide* does it again. This is an indispensable guide for Mac users who want to get started in Photoshop but don't like to read long explanations. The QuickStart way focuses on illustrated, step-by-step examples that cover how to use masks, filters, colors, the new features of Photoshop 3, and more. *$18.00 (264 pages)*

The Photoshop Wow! Book (Mac Edition)
Linnea Dayton and Jack Davis

This book is really two books in one: an easy-to-follow, step-by-step tutorial of Photoshop fundamentals and over 150 pages of tips and techniques for getting the most out of Photoshop version 2.5. Full color throughout, *The Photoshop Wow! Book* includes a disk containing Photoshop filters and utilities. *$35.00 (208 pages, includes disk)*

Protect Your Macintosh
Bruce Schneier

A hands-on guide that discusses all aspects of Macintosh security: backups, viruses, data protection, encryption, network security, and physical security. Includes reviews of useful products that can help you avert or recover from disaster. *$23.95 (350 pages)*

QuarkXPress 3.3: Visual QuickStart Guide (Mac Edition)
Elaine Weinmann

Winner of the 1992 Benjamin Franklin Award, here's a terrific way to get introduced to QuarkXPress. Lots of illustrations and screen shots make each feature of the program absolutely clear. This book is helpful to both beginners and intermediate QuarkXPress users. *$15.95 (240 pages)*

Real World Scanning and Halftones
David Blatner and Steve Roth

Here's a book that will save you time and money as you master the digital halftone process, from scanning images to tweaking them on your Mac to imagesetting them. *$24.95 (275 pages)*

Zap! How Your Computer Can Hurt You and What You Can Do About It
Don Sellers

Learn about the variety of potential hazards of using your computer and how to reduce your risk. Includes chapters on backache, headache, radiation, and much more. *$12.95 (150 pages)*

 For a complete list of Peachpit Press titles call 1-800-283-9444 and request our latest catalog.

Order Form

Qty	Title	Price	Total

Subtotal	
Add applicable state sales tax	
Shipping	
TOTAL	

Shipping .... **UPS Ground**

First Item .... **$ 4**

Each Additional .... **$ 1**

Name

Company

Address

City   State   Zip

Phone   Fax

❏ Check enclosed   ❏ Visa   ❏ MasterCard   ❏ AMEX

Company purchase order #

Credit card #   Exp. Date

What other books would you like us to publish?

Please tell us what you thought of this book:

To order, call:

(800) 283-9444 or

(510) 548-4393 or

(510) 548-5991 (fax)

Peachpit Press

2414 Sixth Street

Berkeley, CA • 94710

MAC